681
Lexington
Avenue

A Beat Education
in New York City
1947–1954

681
Lexington
Avenue
A Beat Education
in New York City
1947–1954

Elizabeth Von Vogt

with a Foreword by Nancy M. Grace

Ten O'Clock Press
a divison of Greater Midwest Publishing
Wooster, Ohio

2008

Ten O'Clock Press, a division of Greater Midwest Publishing, LLC.
P.O. Box 482 Wooster, Ohio 44691
www.greatermidwestpublishing.com

ISBN 978-1-59098-301-0

Library of Congress Control Number: 2008926195
Publisher's Cataloging in Publication Data
Von Vogt, Elizabeth, 1932–
681 Lexington Avenue: A Beat Education in New York City 1947–1954/Elizabeth Von Vogt;
with a foreword by Nancy M. Grace.
ISBN 9781590983010

Cover Photo (front): "Elizabeth Holmes with Kitty on the Rooftop of 681 Lexington Avenue, 1949" by Elizabeth Von Vogt
Cover Collage (front clockwise): "Allen Ginsberg/ Photo Booth Strip, 1950" by the Allen Ginsberg Trust; "Elizabeth Von Vogt, 1954" by Elizabeth Von Vogt; "John Holmes, 1943" by Betty Holmes; "Jack Kerouac/ Mill Valley, California, 1956" by Walter Lehrman
Cover Photo (back): "681 Lexington" by Tom L. Milligan, 2007
Cover Design (front and back): Sarah Walsh

Prologue: Sperr, Percy Louis. "Manhattan: 56th Street—Lexington Avenue." Photographic Views of New York City, 1870s–1970s. June 17, 1940. Photograph. Milstein Division of United States History, Local History & Geneaology, The New York Public Library, Astor, Lenox and Tilden Foundations.

Chapter 1: Sperr, Percy Louis. "Manhattan: 56th Street—Lexington Avenue." Photographic Views of New York City, 1870s–1970s. June 17, 1940. Photograph. Milstein Division of United States History, Local History & Geneaology, The New York Public Library, Astor, Lenox and Tilden Foundations.

Chapter 2: Gottscho-Schleisner, Inc. "Pine St., New York City. II." 1945. Courtesy of The Library of Congress, Prints and Photographs Division, Gottscho-Schleisner Collecton [reproduction number LC-G612-T-48009].

Chapter 3: Gottscho, Samuel H. "New York City Views. Brooklyn Bridge, and lower New York, from Robert Gair Building II." 1932. Courtesy of The Library of Congress, Prints and Photographs Division, Gottscho-Schleisner Collection [reproduction number LC-G612-T01-17799-A].

Chapter 4: Gottscho-Schleisner, Inc. "New York City Views. Skyline from Welfare Island, under bridge." 1950. Courtesy of The Library of Congress, Prints and Photographs Divisions, Gottscho-Schleisner Collection [reproduction number, LC-G613-T-56733].

Chapter 5: Gottscho, Samuel H. "New York City Views. Washington Square I." 1932. Courtesy of The Library of Congress, Prints and Photographs Division, Gottscho-Schleisner Collection [reproduction number LC-G612-66712].

Chapter 6: Gottscho-Schleisner, Inc. "Rockefeller Center, New York City. Planted with azaleas II." 1945. Courtesy of The Library of Congress, Prints and Photographs Division, Gottscho-Schleisner Collection [reproduction number LC-G602-CT-[039]].

Chapter 7: Gottscho-Schleisner, Inc. "City Investing Co., Inc., 30 Broad St., New York City. 91st and Madison Ave. II." 1946. Courtesy of The Library of Congress, Prints and Photographs Division, Gottscho-Schleisner Collection [reproduction number LC-G612-T-48524].

Chapter 8: Gottscho-Schleisner, Inc. "Mrs. John Kean, residence at 863 Lexington Ave., New York City. Exterior." 1944. Courtesy of The Library of Congress, Prints and Photographs Division, Gottscho-Schleisner Collection [reproduction number, LC-G612-T01-45337].

Chapter 9: Gottscho, Samuel H. "New York City Views. New York at night, night view, south, from RCA Building, horizontal." 1933. Courtesy of The Library of Congress, Photographs and Prints Division, Gottscho-Schleisner Collection, [reproduction number LC-G612-T01-20945].

Chapter 10: Gottscho-Schleisner, Inc. "Manny Wolf's Restaurant, 49th St. and 3rd Ave., New York City. General view. 1953. Courtesy of The Library of Congress, Photographs and Prints Division, Gottscho-Schleisner Collection, [reproduction number LC-G613-T-62907].

Chapter 11: "125th Street and Broadway Station (Formerly Manhattan Street). Platforms and Tracks on Manhattan Valley Viaduct." Interborough Rapid Transit Subway, New York, New York County, NY. ca. 1968. Courtesy of The Library of Congress, Photographs and Prints Division, Historic American Engineering Record, [reproduction number HAER NY, 31-NEYO, 86-30].

Chapter 12: Sperr, Percy Louis. "Manhattan: 56th Street—Lexington Avenue." Photographic Views of New York City, 1870s–1970s. June 17, 1940. Photograph. Milstein Division of United States History, Local History & Geneaology, The New York Public Library, Astor, Lenox and Tilden Foundations.

Epilogue: Gottscho-Schleisner, Inc. "New York City Views. Skyline from sixth floor, Welfare Hospital." 1950. Courtesy of The Library of Congress, Prints and Photographs Division, Gottscho-Schleisner Collection [reproduction number, LC-G613-T-56734].

Dedication

To John
for the past

To Julie, Carl, Mark and Jerome, Lourdes, Patti
for now

To Tom, Mike, Katie, Matt, Liz, Jack
for tomorrow

One Gnostic reading of the Garden of Eden reverses the values of the Tree of Knowledge and the Tree of Life as given in *Genesis*.

"For their (the Archons, lower powers who rule our world) tree was appointed as a 'tree of life.' Its root is bitter, its branches are shadows of death, its leaves hatred and deception, its sap . . . is a balm of wickedness and its fruit the desire of death . . .

Over against this the 'tree of knowledge of good and evil' is the insight (*epinoia*) of light, 'because of which they (Archons) gave command *not* to eat of it, that is, not to listen to it, since the command is directed against him (Adam), that he may not look upwards to his perfection . . . his understanding will become sober and he will be like gods since he knows the difference which exists between good and evil men . . .'"

—*Gnosis: The Nature and History of Gnosticism*
Kurt Rudolph

Holmes' pad (4C at 681 Lexington Avenue) was like Grand Central Station with characters dropping in at all hours of the day and night. On one of my visits, I found Kerouac sleeping on the floor and Holmes and his wife wondering what to do with the body.

—*Rebel Without Applause*
Jay Landesman

Table of Contents

Acknowledgements

I would like to thank a few people who were instrumental in furthering this book from its creation to its publication. I am indebted to Ann Charters who wanted to interview me in depth for the biography of John Clellon Holmes that she and Sam Charters are writing. It was she who provided the incentive to develop this memoir. Her husband Sam has always been encouraging of my writing in general. His enthusiasm is infectious. Sterling Lord, my agent for this work, was excited about the book from the beginning and kept it alive in the publishing world in New York.

Jay Landesman, one of John Holmes's oldest friends, supported the book from the start and handled it in London. His editor, Pam Hardyment, followed his lead and sent the manuscript to Kevin Ring, editor of *Beat Scene Magazine*, who very soon proposed publishing the chapters on John and Jack Kerouac as separate pieces— one as a chapbook, the other in the magazine. His enthusiasm led me to Nancy Grace, my editor, without whom the book would not see the light. Her deep and steady appreciation has seen me through fallow times. Her strong response to the manuscript and her hard work has brought it to fruition.

Daniela Platania wrote an astute thesis on John and Jack for her doctorate, and her ideas on their relative place in the Beat canon have influenced my thinking about them. I hope that someday this thesis can be translated from the Italian and published in English. It would add immensely to the scholarship on the Beats.

I would like to thank Dave Moore for making a crucial factual correction in the manuscript. And to Tom Milligan and Mark Von Vogt for taking excellent photos of the new 681 Lexington Avenue.

Finally, without the constant and indomitable support of my husband, Carl, my writing life might have died on the vine.

Foreword

"The fundamental requirement of hot jazz is relaxed cooperation between the performers. The best music usually comes out when each man has the greatest freedom for improvisation within the harmonic framework of the piece being played."[1] The same can be said about a life, and if we replace "man" with "woman," this passage from the August 24, 1947 *New York Times* expresses the philosophy underlying Elizabeth Holmes Von Vogt's memoir of coming of age in the company of her older brother John Clellon Holmes (1926-1988) in post-World War II New York City. The harmonic, although at times raucous and dangerous, structure of the Holmes family in the tattered confines of a fifth-floor flat in Manhattan provided teenage Liz the license to improvise a life. "Yes," she tells us, "John taught me to bring nothing to the table, to put up no barriers, to be blank and fearless, and to learn."

Von Vogt's brother wrote the first novel to chronicle what we now know as the Beat generation, which since its inception in the late forties has fascinated the American public with its wild intellectualism, lyrical Emersonian independence, and gritty anti-establishment verve. Published in 1952, *Go* is a roman à clef, a novel of social realism that introduced the world to a group of intriguing young people—World War II veterans, jazz musicians and enthusiasts, drug addicts, petty criminals, and sexual libertines that included artists and muses such as Jack Kerouac, Allen Ginsberg, and Neal Cassady. Within a few years, these men would emerge whole cloth as creators of a new American Renaissance in cultural and literary history. *Go* still captivates readers. And not only because of its connections to

---

1. Carter Harman. "New Jazz Trends in Night Clubs." *The New York Times*, Section 2, X 5, August, 24, 1947.

these rebel figures but also because it so bravely describes America in transition: the effects of World War II, racism, sexism, national hope and despair. Von Vogt had the advantage of spending her formative years, 1947–1954, in the midst of this rarified world, unknowingly at first and then with calculated enthusiasm, absorbing every bit of wisdom offered to her by this unorthodox "faculty" of writers, artists, secretaries, and overall misfits. Using the genre of memoir, Von Vogt shifts the historical lens to reveal their world through the eyes of a teenager searching for her identity in a middle-class family character- ized by political debate, artistic radicalism, and a spirit of tolerance.

Hers is a world centered on family relationships. She adores her big brother who teaches her about literature and jazz. She cherishes her mother, a divorcée who found herself having to take clerical jobs to support her family. She admires her sister-in-law, who provides sisterly hugs of affirmation. Her world centers on high school and college, both populated by World War II veterans taking advantage of GI Bill payments offering up to $500 per school year for tuition and books, plus a monthly subsistence allowance.[2] Hers is a world of teen crushes, sexual experimentation, neighborhood delis with major film stars as regulars, weekly trips to baseball games, radios and record players, un-air-conditioned apartments, and the long-lost art of whistling to your favorite tunes—hers included Wardell Gray and Dexter Gordon's "The Hunt" and "The Chase." But Von Vogt also lived in a world of Communist intrigue, tabooed interracial relation- ships, grimy bars populated by fist-fights and cheap beer, lecherous professors, young adult alcoholics, and the ever-present fear of the bomb. Perhaps more than anything, it is a world in which a young woman who never quite fit in learns that while everyone is some-

2. Editor's Note: Approximately 15 million veterans returned to civilian life, including 250,000 Blacks. From 1945 to 1947, New York City saw its population increase by almost 700,000 veterans, many of whom took advantage of the GI benefits under Public Law 346. The legisla- tion also provided unemployment and housing benefits. For the entire country, the investment totaled $14.5 billion. See Normal Polmar, *World War II: America at War 1941–1945*, New York: Random House, 1991; *The Simon and Schuster Encyclopedia of World War II*, New York: Simon & Schuster, 1978; and *Population of New York City 1940–1948*, New York: Consolidated Edison Company of New York, Inc.: 1948.

body's monster, the soul can be restored in one's memory of a special place—hers is 681 Lexington Avenue. Von Vogt's vision of this sanctuary is quintessentially postindustrial Beat. Instead of squelching the generative powers of nature, her urban landscape effects a frontier that, as writer Robert Bennett describes, enables "a free poetic life and new hinterlands for the aesthetic imagination."[3]

Interestingly, Von Vogt does not present herself as what we have come to know as the female Beat stereotype: the silent girl who wore black. Granted, she struggles with silence—it embarrasses yet protects her. But it is more accurately the silence of any young sibling, especially a female, who adores her older, self-confident, loquacious brother. It is not the male Beat silence of cultural and personal ennui or the silence of the Beat female trying to emulate the masculine persona. And she clearly saw no need to wear the Beat female costume, the striking black tights, tops, and skirts, all without girdle or bra. Instead, we meet a teenage bobby-soxer who seems more comfortable in swing-era clothes.

So with respect to costume, an important signifier of any cultural movement, we might question her links to and affiliation with Beat. But when we do, we must remember that "Beat" is a vexed, unstable term. Yes, it can mean worn out or discarded, but it can also mean perfect happiness and peace as in "beatific," and it can mean rebellious, jazzy, and experimental in terms of one's life and/or one's literary style. There is no agreed-upon definition, even amongst those who coined the term, and thus we stand on firmest ground when we conclude that what makes someone Beat is an association with a historical moment and social context in which one turns to a bohemian community in order to reject specific cultural practices and beliefs characterizing cold war repressions. With this understanding, we can recognize the Beat school from which Von Vogt graduated, the way in which its curriculum shaped her as an independent and imaginative mind.

---

3. Bennett, Robert. *Deconstructing Post-World War II New York City: The Literature, Art, Jazz, and Architecture of an Emerging Global Capital.* New York: Routledge, 2003.

Perhaps not surprisingly, Von Vogt has chosen to tell her story via a genre associated with women in the Beat movement. Memoirs written about the early years of the Beat generation have been authored almost exclusively by women, beginning with Diane di Prima's campy *Memoirs of a Beatnik* in 1969 and extending up to Edie Kerouac-Parker's posthumously published *You'll Be Okay: My Life With Jack Kerouac* (constructed and edited by Timothy Moran, 2007). It was Joyce Johnson's memoir *Minor Characters*, which won the National Book Critics Award in 1983, that finally brought the role of women in the movement to national attention. The Beat generation was dominated by men, especially in its literary guise, and the women, be they sisters as was Von Vogt, or girlfriends or wives, were long invisible, not only to the general public but also to the academy that has only recently begun to consider seriously their presence and importance. As a consequence, many of the women no doubt saw themselves, and were recognized by others, as more fitting subjects for a form of historical prose than any other genre.

Memoir has a long history as a female-focused genre and thus an unfortunate reputation as a subordinate or inferior form of history relied upon by those with lesser power and talents. It was rejected by the male Beats who preferred the roman à clef, autobiographical poetry, essay, science fiction, or the screenplay, although ironically Kerouac himself conflated genres to the extent that many of his mature works, such as *Desolation Angels* (1965), *Some of the Dharma* (posthumously 1995), and *Vanity of Duluoz* (1968), project a distinctly memoir-like quality. Consequently, it is legitimate to claim that our present-day fascination with memoir, which has finally achieved a more elevated critical status as both the documentation and the creation of personal and cultural truths, can be credited to Beat writers such as Kerouac who moved literature in a fresh direction.

Memoir, then, focusing on a relatively short period in one's life, as opposed to autobiography that attempts to capture the panoramic rather than a snapshot, seems an ideal vehicle of expression for women like Von Vogt who were associated with figures such as Kerouac, Ginsberg, and Clellon Holmes. In memoir, they establish their own authority, first through a focus on their intimate relationships with these cultural heroes and next through their ability to tell a compelling story about them. In *681*, we see Von Vogt doing just that, crafting extended and touching portraits of her brother and Kerouac, while giving us insightful glimpses of Ginsberg and Cassady as well as non-Beat figures including political philosopher Gene Sharp and film scholar Robert Gessner. Finally, memoir allows women like Von Vogt to transcend the conventions of the genre itself, as Ronna Johnson explains, by providing them a tool with which to tell "their own Beat tales outside their colonization by Beat literature."[4] In other words, by claiming the memoir as their own territory, intentionally or not, Von Vogt and the Beat memoirists who preceded her further their subjectivity in the public record of the Beat movement, simultaneously reconfiguring the Beat canon to include their own voices while helping readers better understand American postwar literary and social history.

Von Vogt's memoir is almost a historical novel as much as it is a memoir. She plays with point of view by beginning with a chapter composed from the perspective of her younger self, only fourteen years old. The bulk of the narrative that follows is a translation of the era mediated by Von Vogt's contemporary eye: vivid present-tense descriptions and scenes of people and events throughout; language that blends fifties slang with Beat and bop argot; and jazz-inspired rhythms created with em dashes, coordinating conjunctions, staccato and elliptical phrasing, fragments, and jump cuts. Memoirs such as Joyce Johnson's and Hettie Jones's *How I Became Hettie Jones* (1990) function similarly, overtly acknowledging the literary qualities and materials with which any self creates her story. However, these latter two never lose sight of their historical referent, of their implied duty to comment on the present through the story of the past. *681*, in contrast, relies upon minimal scaffolding to remind us of the temporal distance between actual events and Von Vogt's narrating of them.

---

4. Nancy M. Grace and Ronna C. Johnson, *Breaking the Rule of Cool: Reading and Interviewing Women Beat Writers*. Jackson, Mississippi: University Press of Mississippi, 2005, 37-38.

Readers will frequently find themselves in the moment with the Von Vogt of her own memory, expected to know the streets of Manhattan and the dozens of jazz musicians that have become American musical history.[5] In this respect, the memoir aligns itself with di Prima's *Memoirs of a Beatnik* (1969) and Brenda "Bonnie" Frazer's *Troia: Mexican Memoirs* (1969), both of which engage in stylistic word play and collapse time and characters sufficiently to undermine the author/referent dyad upon which memoir as history depends. *681* bridges these two extremes of literary practice, avoiding the tired memoir trope of non-reflective reportage focused solely on facticity.

Of course, in the process, *681* offers bildungsroman-universal themes, the realization that people across decades are never really all that different after all. But, in truth, Von Vogt's story isn't any more enlightening than many other works of fiction about the same general period, such as Alix Kates Shulman's *Memoirs of an Ex-Prom Queen* (1972), Sylvia Plath's *The Bell Jar* (1963 under pseudonym Victoria Lucas), Grace Metallious's *Peyton Place* (1956), Herman Wouk's *Marjorie Morningstar* (1955), and Joyce Johnson's *Come and Join the Dance* (1962). Neither does it differ drastically from Jones, Johnson, di Prima, Frazer, or even Carolyn Cassady and Edie Kerouac-Parker's memoirs. To whatever degree of artistic success, all of these augment our still-evolving understanding of mid-twentieth-century America, women's roles in that history, and the reality of Beat as a cultural phenomenon. To its credit, *681* does not try to be particularly different, to make that leap and rely on overt articulations of universality to keep itself afloat. Instead it attempts an honest description and illumination of postwar bohemian New York City. In its modest and personal vision, the memoir casts a wide net, just as did the Beats themselves.

—Nancy M. Grace

5. Editor's Note: To assist readers who may feel uncomfortable in this space, we have included a small set of clarifying footnotes as well as an extensive glossary of names.

Introduction

This introduction grew out of a series of interviews with Elizabeth Von Vogt conducted by Nancy M. Grace in October and November 2007.

681 is a loving work about the unconventional Beat life with all the sensations and feelings that I could get out of that rather crazy teenage world. It felt normal to me—the older kids and all the vets in New York and our fifth-floor walk up. The entire experience was "crazy." However, my feelings about it were positive, and I wanted to show that you can write about a life that on paper doesn't sound good at all, but if you've gotten something out of it, you can express how truly fertile and promising it was. So many memoirs are about all the horrible things that make people unhappy, but with the kind of life I had, I can see that I was quite happy. Often lonely, lonesome, but basically happy. I *got* stuff out of it. It was a daily dose of discovery. My brother John later said to me, years after the Beat era was over, "I used to wonder if you'd survive. I'm really amazed that you got through it." He could see that it was not the ideal life for a teenage girl. And I too could see that it was a bizarre life: you wouldn't want your fourteen-year-old daughter living with cockroaches and beginning to sleep around and go to bars and drink—and yet it was rich with stimulation. I realized that more than ever after completing the memoir.

I composed the first chapter at least ten years ago, wanting to tell my mother's story—how she was divorced and lived in New York with a teenage daughter and on the margin of poverty. Then I thought that New York in the late forties and fifties would be interesting, that people should know more about that. So I began the book again from that angle and then dropped it. It just didn't seem to carry me any place at that point. It wasn't really about me. The catalyst for returning to the memoir was Ann Charters, who asked to interview me for the biography she is writing about John. The best way for me to talk to her about my memories of John was to write down everything about the relationship that I had with him. I really wrote the narrative for Charters, knowing that I could write better than I can talk.

So I just kept writing, and it just kept evolving, and the memories became their own story as I went along. The process took about six months. I'd found a subject to write about that involved me but was bigger than myself and even bigger than postwar New York in the forties and fifties. An important aspect of memoir is for it to ramify out beyond the personal—which is, after all, only the stone thrown in the water. I don't know if I could have written *681* if I hadn't begun to see that I was involved with the Beats through my brother John.

He's very important. His novels *Go* and *The Horn* could eventually loom as seminal Beat books with a broader than Beat resonance. Scholars are beginning to see this. For instance, Daniela Platania, an Italian literary critic, in her doctoral thesis "John Clellon Holmes and Jack Kerouac: Revelation Is Revolution," compares *Go* and *On the Road* (The Beat chronicles) and then *The Horn* and *The Subterraneans* (the Beat and Black experience). I can read Italian, having studied it for seven years, and as I read her conclusion it's that Jack Kerouac was the revolution but he needed a revealer: John was that—he delivered the revelation of that revolution. A number of the Beats kept marginalizing John, saying he wasn't one of them (and he didn't live like them), but without his introduction of them to the world in *Go* and even *The Horn*, there would be no perspective beyond their own involved voices.

Writing *681* also enabled me to see that that period was very influential in my own life. John once said, and he was quoting someone, "Your basic long full-life attitudes are all shaped before you're twenty-five." In this case, I thought, "Yes, this story takes me up to twenty-one, and these were the things that probably influenced my whole life." My basic attitudes were largely shaped by John, listening to John, living that entire seven-year period around John. From

John and New York and the whole experience, I gained a great deal of knowledge at a very high level that I couldn't use then. New York in the fifties was exciting mentally for a budding, intellectual kid. I never did get along very well when I was in a suburban situation. I always felt ill at ease. But in New York life was exciting, it was fun. There was submersion not only in the arts but also in the life of the streets—always so much to do. My New York life centered on reading and learning and listening to my brother. It was fascinating.

My recent thinking about Gnosticism has helped me understand how I could see this period in my life, which is why I begin *681* with an epigraph about Gnosticism, especially the Tree of Knowledge and the Tree of Life. In the Gnostic traditions, the Tree of Knowledge is the good one. That's a paradox that occurred to me. (John talked about that—and Ginsberg was also interested in Gnosticism, as well as the mysticism of Kabbalah.) The knowledge period was great for me, and then living began—the Tree of Life—with its taint and confusion.

So I found myself in the memoir mired in paradox. But I find ambiguity in everything and am drawn to the contradictory. For instance, Bill Cannastra comes across in *Go* as a real demon, but to me, as I listened to John talk about him, the dark figure emerged with a wondrous energy and excitement. Like the masturbating man across the way from my window that I include in the memoir, all these "bad things" carried an aura of excited discovery. Paradox? The secret of my New York life.

The Beats—and myself too—felt as though they were living in a Dostoyevskean world—existential and imminent with prophecy. The high intensity of drama and revelation all through Dostoyevsky— the dark garrets in St. Petersburg—were like rainy New York in the late forties. The party scenes in *Go* often slavishly reek of "Dusty's" scenes. Everybody's life is always being overturned by revelation.

D.H. Lawrence, with his burning need for sexual renewal in a dead world, also appears in the memoir as an important influence on myself and the Beats. I remember Jack and John talking of Lawrence—long talks, when they would be shouting at each other about Lawrencian revelations. They saw him as a great prophet of new sexuality, the rebirth of men and women in a new way. They were into sex and spirituality, and I heard things at fifteen that I didn't understand but felt the power of—like John saying, "Sex is the only place left to reveal our real choice, our real humanity." Lawrence saw the industrial world as killing the feelings. The flesh was all of possible purity left. Well, John, Jack and the Beats took off from that and proclaimed sex (Neal Cassady as muse here) as the last source of energy left to transform that lousy materialistic America of the forties and fifties. They talked a lot about *The Plumed Serpent*, which is now *not* one of my favorite Lawrences, but at that time I thought it must have been the Bible because they considered it the greatest book about men and women and sex and, of course, Mexico, the mecca of the fellaheen earth.

Race is a basic theme of the memoir, and New York in the late forties and early fifties was on the frontier of race relations. The city was a capital of baseball with three major league teams and the first black players to play in the majors. I loved baseball, which I write about in *681*, especially the Brooklyn Dodgers: Jackie Robinson, Roy Campenella, Gene Hermanski, PeeWee Reese, Duke Snider. I kept lists of all the players and every team, collected some cards, and listened to all the games on the radio in the afternoon. My girlfriend also loved baseball, and we went to games all the time. We used to sit in the bleachers behind Duke Snider, who was in center field. I don't remember any girls except my one girlfriend liking baseball. I'm sure the others didn't care a damn about it. But to me Ebbets Field was the frontline of a revolution, a place where race barriers were breached and the new world had arrived—so that I could cheer Jackie Robinson just as I did Duke Snider. There Margaret and I felt the frisson of liberation, and it was intoxicating. New York again.

But more than anything, as I try to convey in the memoir, I wanted to live the life my brother had lived. The Beats—John, Jack, Allen—were artists. I became a teacher after graduating in 1954 from New York University with a double major in English and history, but I didn't like teaching very much. In my first year, I was very irresponsible. I didn't organize well, I didn't have a syllabus. I was single until I was thirty-one, having affairs, traveling, learning about many things, and teaching was just a way to make a living. When I got married, that solved a lot of problems and I could start teaching with more interest. But in my twenties, teaching did foster a nomadic life which suited the Beat approach to living, which I had obviously ingested from 681.

681 records the real and factual, but it reads like the fiction I write. The roman à clef, the style of *Go*, is a perfectly traditional and very common fictional form. For a memoir, though, the most important thing is to tell the emotional truth, and then to tell as much of the factual truth as you can grab hold of. You owe something to the facts, to be as true as you can to them, but the memoir is an emotional book, and you have to get at the truth of your emotions and feelings. It's not an autobiography, which is more sequential, historical, and repetitive. Memoir is an emotional thing about a segment of life that was rife with feeling, revelation, and meaning.

Writing the memoir wasn't hard or painful, as it is for some. I have changed the names of certain individuals, giving them pseudonyms to protect their privacy, and I had to conduct research to verify some factual aspects, for instance, the text about Robert Gessner in the film department at New York University. Even though I remembered it very well, I had to be sure. But when I called NYU and the film department, the people I spoke with had never heard of Gessner. So I went to the library archives, where I confirmed that Gessner was real. He was head of the department and the first person to start a film school in the East. It turned out I was right. I also reviewed a few photographs from the time period. The one photograph of me that I describe in detail in the memoir I hadn't looked at before I wrote about it. But it was exactly the way I had remembered it. I also looked through a lot of my old photograph albums from that period. It's a memory thing; sometimes it's there, and sometimes it's not. But the memoir must be anchored in the affective memory.

Some readers may recognize that I've already written this story from my mother's perspective in *The Adventures of Dorothy and Marian*.[6] Dorothy is my mother, and Marian is my counterpoint in the narrative; it seemed like the only way for me to get out of my life then and truly, compassionately, get into my mother's head. It was fiction—an effort of imagination, a stretch to recreate—from actual facts as I knew them—another person's unique experience written twenty years later. John wrote about that whole part of his life in *Go*. So there are three versions of 681 Lexington in the late forties and fifties. *681* is mine.

I can understand where memoirists get the idea that they want to write—to prove that "my life has integrity." Everyone's life, I suppose, forms a kind of whole. But how to find that whole? The Beats, like John, Jack, and Allen, were artists after all. It's the job of writers to discover and maybe even create their integrity—to find the form that integrates our lives along with theirs as example. Everyone has a story, a little chink of life that they find emotional meaning in. But memoirists have to do more—they have to present their emotional integrity in a way that ripples outward to whoever is out there—to almost make a myth of the life—like Jack did in his Duluoz Legend. I like to think John would agree. But he would talk a perfect essay out of it.

I'd also like to think John and my mother would approve and believe they got a pretty good deal from me in *681*. It's obvious how much I looked up to John and how inspiring he was in those days, at least up in 5D. Strange, though, that my portrait of him doesn't cohere with his self-portrait in *Go*. Perspective again. He might not like the end where I am cynical about the trendy crowd that he later consorted with in Saybrook, Connecticut, on weekends. But John obviously had all kinds of doubts about that life and the people, the Beats, of '48 and '49. I, however, only saw the excited and exploring John, a better picture of him than he gives us in *Go*. I can't think,

---

6. Editor's Note: *The Adventures of Dorothy and Marian* was published by the Writers Club Press in 2000.

though, that they'd object, other than to say that both pictures are incomplete—doesn't everybody in somebody else's books feel his incompleteness? It's finally always a clash of perspectives.

But this is my emotional truth as far as I can resurrect it and connect it to the wider world of its time and place. And I hope that it records at least a part of others' truths—others who made me so much of what I am, and to whom I live largely in gratitude.

Nobleboro, Maine,
March 2008

681
Lexington
Avenue

A Beat Education
in New York City
1947–1954

Prologue

Snapshots of a Pre-Beat Summer
A Fourteen-Year-Old's Story

——— Mom and I are breaking up house. We have to leave our big room on the sixth floor of East Fortieth Street. I like this room with its front wall of windows that look across to the apartments on the south side of the street. I've played hooky a lot from school and stayed home listening to the radio while mom and my big sister go to work, and I look in those windows across the way and imagine lives—the blond woman in her robe opening the curtains, the man standing at the window fixing his tie. I enjoy visiting our neighbor in her tiny room across the hall that faces north where I can stare at the Chrysler Building and think of my uncle who works in an advertising office right under its silver point.

My older sister's been living with us, but her husband has just returned from the war, and the two of them are heading someplace West (Mom says they have a scheme to open a motel). So we're looking for someplace else affordable. Everybody says that it's impossible to find an apartment these days. There's nothing in the paper, and people are grabbing at ones they hear about through friends, acquaintances, or co-workers. The place is crawling with people looking for studios, one bedrooms, walk-ups, railroads, and sublets. With the war over and the UNO[1] out on Long Island, it's as if all roads lead to New York. What a mad scramble!

I'm glad that eighth grade is over and Mom doesn't plan to send me back there to Friends Seminary in the fall. In fact, we don't have any plans for fall. My mother's clerical job is shaky, and she's worried about getting by on the alimony from my father. "It's hard to find an apartment, Lizzie—at least anything we can afford. If we don't find something soon we may have to go up to Chappaqua to house keep for the Harrises."

But I want to stay here, and I leap for joy when my big brother, John, and his wife, Marian, dig up a one-bedroom sublet on Lexington Avenue between Fifty-sixth and Fifty-seventh streets. They are living in a four-room coldwater railroad flat up on East Eighty-ninth in Yorkville and pay $25 a month and cook their food on a hot plate and take baths in the kitchen. It's a fine place for John to write while Marian works—another clerical job. (It seems that New York is swarming with women working at filing and typing and making $35 a week.) They're having a lot of fun too, as far as I can tell. They party every week with a painter, Alan Wood-Thomas, and a writer, Alan Harrington, across the street. They've heard about the Lexington Avenue apartment through the grapevine, and I think they want us to hold it for them for the fall when their lease is up on Eighty-ninth. The new flat is heated with a real bathroom, and the living room is big with nice molding around the ceiling and parquet floors and great French windows facing Lexington Avenue. But it's $45 a month, and it's going to be a squeeze. Marian says they'll scrounge to pay the rent, though, because, as she tells me, "We've been cold and primitive for a year and that's long enough!"

---

1. Editor's Note: UNO is an abbreviation for United Nations Organization, which came into existence on Oct. 24, 1945. By the 1950s, people were referring to as simply the UN. In its earliest days, the UN moved frequently, the General Assembly meeting in London and Flushing New York in 1946. The Security Council met in London in January 1946 and then in Hunter College, the Henry Hudson Hotel, and Lake Success on Long Island the rest of the year.

★★★★

It's June 1946, and we move uptown to apartment 4C, 681 Lexington, and I'm in heaven. I'm falling in love with this place and can't conceive of being anywhere else. I've had happy times before—playing every day in a pool in Altadena, California, one summer; sledding down a long, scary hill in Jersey; tagging along behind my brother and his gang; and walking my favorite dog. But this summer I'm fourteen, and for the first time that I can remember, real fun comes bouncing off the streets. It rushes into me from the racket of the "D" train sliding into the station at Fifty-third Street, and it thrills me as I look west to the strange pointy tower of a warehouse—something Chinese or Arabian—before I run down the stairs to the subway.

It's hot everywhere this summer. In the old days, I would have given anything to spend my day in a pool, a lake, Long Island Sound, the ocean. But this year, I'm only too glad to swim in the hot air of the city. It shimmers and pulses like a giant hot heart outside my window. My poor mother—a little heavy and in her forties—suffers. She's sweating and fanning herself while a fire engine shrieks by below the windows—they do it a couple of times a day—and the roaches crawl around the crumbs by the hot plate. She's disappointed and probably worried. But I like it all soft and scorching—shirts open, legs bare—all the activity of the streets—everything boiling up with promise, a steaming secret purpose in the air. Manhattan gives me such a happy buzz just tramping through its streets that I tell my mother when she proposes an outing to Jones Beach or Coney Island, "No, Mom, I don't want to ever leave the island of Manhattan."

★ ★ ★ ★

I'm having the time of my life. And it all turns around music.

John has given me his old turntable. He and Marian have bought a new one—big, with a cover and a real speaker built in. But his old one will serve and is the best present anyone has ever given me. I've put it on a small table in front of the window in the bedroom, which my mother has graciously given to me. It's a small room, so the single cot is close by and I can perch on it and look out the window at the offices on the second and third floors across the street—big rooms with wide drafting tables and piles of cartons stacked all around. And I play music.

Here's my daily schedule:

After my mother leaves for work, I dress. I wear a big pleated print skirt that swings low below the knees. All the girls are wearing them. I go two blocks down the street to a small record shop where I can buy a little box of fifty steel needles for a quarter. I get a dollar or so allowance every week, so I can usually buy one ten-inch 78 record a week for about seventy-five cents. I used to listen to Martin Block's Saturday morning swing show on the radio and grew up on swing bands. When we lived in New Jersey, Mom and I would sometimes go with John to Sunday night jazz concerts at New York's Town Hall. We'd come over the Hudson on the bus from Englewood, arcing high on the George Washington Bridge. I'd stomp and scream at the "all-out" jam sessions that finished the concert. There they'd all be together—my future beat-up New York heroes—Muggsy Spanier, Max Kaminsky, Pee Wee Russell, Georg Brunis, Bobby Hackett, Bud Freeman, Jess Stacy, George Wettling, Brad Gowans, Miff Mole, Eddie Condon. But *now* I live on the island with them—just a walk or subway ride from where they play every night—at Nick's in the Village, Jimmy Ryan's on Fifty-second Street. Now with a walk to Fifty-fourth Street, a box of needles for the heavy tone arm, and a black shellac disc with a red Commodore label, I can own them.

I begin buying those Commodores one at a time—"Ballin' the Jack," "Ja-da," "Love Is Just Around the Corner." I go home and play them, first the one, then the two, three, and four that begin my collection. For the rest of the morning, I play them over and over again. Then I make a sandwich, and with some lunch money, I go downstairs and next door to the Dover Delicatessen to buy a piece of cheesecake. If I'm lucky I may see somebody famous at the counter where everybody yells and barks out orders and you can't be shy or you'll never get your food. Last week I saw the actor Montgomery Clift, thin and incredibly handsome and very quiet and sure of himself. He got waited on with a smile and a "Mr. Clift, what's it today?" I've heard he lives over on Fifty-sixth Street between Lex and Park.

After lunch, I go to the corner to buy a newspaper—the *PM*[2]. My mom introduced me to this leftist evening paper. Life seems to be floating on the edges of a revolutionary world, caught passively in the vortex of historical forces. There are those Communist Harrises she may have us living with in the fall and odd friends of theirs who may visit here sometime this summer. I'm just beginning to wake up to world events, and somehow it seems natural (though it's probably not) in this crazy yelling town of people, who appear to say and do most everything they want to do and don't care what anybody thinks, to begin taking a left-handed approach to world history. I'm beginning to take a stand on the world stage—one that seems to grow naturally out of these chaotic, anarchic, promising streets. So I read *PM* in the afternoon—Max Lerner, definitely, but even more, Max Werner, who is stronger and even leftier.

Then it's off to my giant warehouse that holds secrets hoards of musical history. No, it's not a little hole in the wall like the ones every few blocks on Lex. It's a whole *department* store of music— the Liberty Music Shop on Madison Avenue and Forty-ninth. The store is large with high ceilings and carpeted floors, and on working afternoons it's crammed with intense, terribly serious young men in short-sleeved shirts—mostly handsome and dark, probably students (the city teems with them), remote boys five years older than me who know everything important about the new ideas I'm just waking up to. In the back of the store there is a small department where they sell foreign records—His Master's Voice. An older man with glasses and a friendly scowl who I negotiate with every week hands

---

2. Editor's Note: *PM* stands for *Picture Magazine*, a daily paper in New York City from 1940 to 1948. Published by Ralph Ingersoll and underwritten by Marshall Field III, *PM* eschewed advertising, was formatted like a newsmagazine, and was considered somewhat leftist, although not as Communist-oriented as the *Daily Worker*.

me the ten-inch disc of "Singin' the Blues" with Bix Beiderbecke and Frankie Trumbauer and asks me if I would like to hear it. He points up the stairs where I travel along a balcony of listening booths—glassed-in, lighted, and each one taken by a serious young man with vacant eyes and head nodding in silence. I find an empty one and put on my record. Alone and in control of magic, I listen to the most beautiful song and solos I've ever heard in my short journey through jazz. Hours and days of it are not enough. I look out the window, and with the pure lonesome tone of Trumbauer's tenor sax, the Manhattan rush hour becomes a river of harmony, strong with loveliness.

Before Mom comes home, there's another hour or two of music—the record of the day over and over: Pee Wee Russell moaning, Max Kaminsky's clarion call, me bouncing on the bed as I watch the men across the way putting on their seersucker jackets and turning off the lights in the offices—the end of the day. But the record goes on and on into the accumulated heat of five o'clock and the swarming, sweaty bodies that gush along the sidewalks below, until I hear my mother's key in the door. My day is complete.

★★★★

New York is dancing on an undercurrent of revolution this summer. I tramp the streets with conspiracy in my heart. All these nice smiling men with suits and briefcases striding up Forty-second Street or down on Wall Street and Broad are going to turn the world upside down. I hear them plotting it in our apartment at 681 Lex:

A cluster of men, and one tall laughing lady, are sitting in my mother's living room. They are all Communists. As usual, it's hot and the French windows are open. Evening noise rises up with the oven air from the street. Traffic, horns, women laughing with loud men, probably high and going in and out of the Venetian Bar downstairs next to the deli. Everybody in here is laughing too—quietly, secretly—as they sip the rum and cokes my mother has served. I'm all ears and feel suddenly as if I'm in on the planning for some mighty cataclysm that will turn this city upside down.

"You know, Bernard, I think the time is right. Lots of anger around—all this Iron Curtain talk. And this 80th Congress![3] Labor's stirred up."

"Perhaps. A few strategic moves on the market and the whole thing could come tumbling down."

"Ah, the summer of revolution."

"Amen, my boy."

The men are jolly—middle-aged in business suits, with ties loosened at the neck, just come from work and "meetings" downtown on Wall Street and somewhere on Forty-second Street. Bernard, a dark, heavyset, pleasant man, and the big laughing lady have an office there. My mother says they are high-priced accountants who own their own business. The lady's husband is here too—also tall, very bald, and with the widest grin I've ever seen. The other, shorter, also bald man is genial, but is very pointed when he talks. The others listen intently. He is the star. He's the husband's brother and is highly placed in the family brokerage firm on Wall Street. They smile at me and are very courteous with my mother, though they don't include her in their conversation, which has a mysterious air of planning about it. Most of the important details seem left unsaid. Kay, the laughing lady with a messy bun of hair, whispered to my mother that she had just gotten her Party membership card. "I'm the last one, Betty. Lem is so proud of me. And Bernard says we're really in business now! Hee, hee!"

They break off to talk about a new book on Franco in Spain, the tyranny of his regime, that I've heard a lot about this summer, *Franco's Black Spain*. I've been nagging my mother to get a copy for me. Then the names "Earl," "Eugene," and "Bob" are tossed around. A German one turns them all quiet and grave. "*Gerhard* is getting in some trouble. By fall we'll probably have to do something, can't afford to have him in jail." They "hmmm" and stop talking, each

---

3. Editor's Note: The 80th Congress met from January 3, 1947, to January 3, 1949. It is probably best known for overriding President Harry Truman's veto of the Taft-Hartley Act, which placed considerable restrictions on the power of labor unions. Truman called the Congress the "Do-Nothing Congress."

seeming to think this over. Then they get ready to leave, thanking my mother. Bernard picks up my *PM* and gives me a kindly, pointed look. "This is a good start, Liz. Soon, though, you'll be ready for the *Daily Worker.* Your mother says you're a real reader and follower of current events. Try the Worker's Bookshop down on Eighth Street."

Lem looks down on the dark, noisy avenue. "Be nice to wake them all up." He grins broadly. "Throw a good *red* monkey wrench into all this New York bourgeois decadence."

As they file out the door, I catch Kay whispering loudly to my mother. (It seems she always whispers with a giggling flourish—she's a jolly spy.) "Hope you and Liz will move up in September. It promises to be such an exciting fall—and we *need* each other. Remember, to each according to his need!"

I do pick up a *Daily Worker* a few days later at the newsstand on Fifty-ninth Street and find it clear and strong and more bracing than *PM.* The bookshop on Eighth Street is piled high with books and magazines, and unnerves me a little with its posters of Lenin and Stalin and the big bearded faces of Marx and Engels. Books on theory and the Soviet Union, on capitalism and dialectical materialism and socialist realism. I buy a copy of the literary magazine *New Masses,* foregoing another Bix record for the week.

★★★★

The last week of a sweltering August—I buy "I'm Coming, Virginia," the last Bix on my list. From four floors up, I'm watching the 4:30 street. The air outside the window is boiling. Men carry their jackets—everybody mops faces and necks. It's hell. But they're rushing just the same—smoking, talking, laughing, and heading into the bars and delis. They stand in line at the bus stop on Fifty-seventh Street and pick up a couple of the four evening papers at the newsstand. The mad dash never stops, and with sweet music blaring in my ear, I can't believe it will *ever* stop. The scruffy man with the organ grinder, the delivery boys with big baskets on their bicycles, the fire engine that screams a wedge through it all. I don't want it to turn over or get better or ever, ever change. Lexington Avenue—a grand river of longing that never stops flowing and never reaches the sea.

★★★★

But it did stop.

It's September, and we have to move in with the Harrises, and I enter Horace Greeley High School in Chappaqua, New York, where I pour over picture books about the Soviet Revolution of 1917 and wait for the second American revolution.

We pick up more nice men at the train station, and I sit and listen in a living room filled with Kay's grand piano and people who now have last names—Robert Thompson, Earl Browder, Harry Bridges, Gus Hall—talk, talk, plan and plan. And the mysterious German man appears. Lem brings him from the station on a round-about route home, while he talks about the FBI and planes overhead, and says across me (there's three of us on the front seat) with a smile, "The time's drawing near, Gerhard. We feel it getting right for the first moves . . . "

By November, they're all toasting Stalin at the Thanksgiving table, and then Gerhard Eisler disappears—only to turn up in East Germany—safe and sound and keeping up the good work, I gather. There had been veiled talk of boats and a lonely beach on Long Island and poof! they pull "it" off. Kay plays a Chopin mazurka loudly one evening, and Lem wanders through the living room humming, so jolly and pleased with themselves and the new world coming.

Me, I spend the fall mourning the old and its capital, Manhattan.

I climb a hill that my sister had shown me when I was a kid. From the top under the high-tension towers I look thirty-nine miles to the south, and when the sky is clear, I can see the Empire State Building and even the RCA[4] sometimes, and I cry.

---

4. Editor's Note: Now the GE Building, the RCA Building, 259 m, was completed in 1933 and is the focal point of Rockefeller Center in Manhattan. RCA stood for Radio Cooperation of America. The Empire State Building at 350 Fifth Avenue is 443.2 m tall.

Chapter 1

Climbing the Tree of Life at 681

—— At fourteen, it's good if you can get your biggest dose of happiness from learning. And you'll learn a hell of a lot more if your school is in a brownstone with no gym and no sports, and your home is a fifth-floor walk-up lacking even a fire escape to sit on to enjoy the sun. At fourteen, my pimply mind, with only a sediment of childish leftism and Commodore Dixieland at the base of its bowl, was parched. At that time, I didn't know how much. I was in the dark until the waters of taste and fact began to pour in.

Thanks to my brother John, my mother and I were able to move back to New York City in January 1947. John had again collared an apartment for us, this time upstairs from his own at 681 Lexington. Ours, 5D, was a fifth floor walk-up in the back with a big skylight slanting up through the roof; one bedroom, smaller than our old one in 4C; and the same hotplate and fridge in the hall and roaches in the tub. We also had a non-working fireplace that became a bookcase for my mother's sacred Eastern texts, one window in a crooked corner of the living room, and a large Tree of Heaven shooting five stories up from the concrete pad below and sending a musty smell into our room on hot summer nights. A grimy sweat poured out of it. It was my closest contact with nature for the next seven years. We lived in 5D until I graduated from New York University in the winter of 1954.

In those years, there were drunks in the hallway, soot and roaches everywhere, and dim bulbs lighting the stairs. A fashionable, plump lady, her made-up daughter, and estranged angry husband screamed and tried to kill each other with knives next door. There was all-night rioting and drinking from the Venetian Bar on the block. There was no doubt about it: 681 Lexington Avenue was a hellhole that both scared and thrilled me—and would continue to scare and thrill me for the next seven years of my life.

Not long after that first day in January 1947, I came home from my first day of school at Rhodes School on Fifty-fourth Street[5]. I remember being met by John and Marian who were painting the small entrance hall that housed the hot plate.

"Well, Liz, how was school?"

John was grinning down at me from the ladder. Yellow paint was spattered everywhere as I squeezed by him. He was cheerful and expected hope from me. Behind his horn-rimmed glasses small lights danced in his eyes. John didn't ask me many questions. Instead he gave long, complicated, beautiful and terrifying answers. At that time in my life, I couldn't yet see how these "answers" would grow and fulminate and stretch branches over my adolescence, a growing tree of knowledge nurturing the runty tree of life I was becoming.

So I stumbled. "It was kind of strange. I walked into a science class, and, well, it was all older guys, like you—even older. A few girls, I guess my age, but all dressed and made-up—looking older too. Gosh, the guys were so *big*!"

"Well," he said coming down the ladder, "that's great, Liz! They're vets. You'll learn as much from them as you will from the teachers."

He saw that I was puzzled and doubtful. "Cheer up. Something different from those usual public schools with boring kids in cliques."

---

5. Editor's Note: Rhodes Preparatory School, which opened in 1912 at 125th Street, relocated to 9-11 West Fifty-fourth Street, between Fifth and Sixth avenues in Manhattan in 1945. This private school was located in what had been the James Goodwin mansion; it remained the Rhodes School until 1979. The building is now owned by the United States Trust Company of New York and serves as a bank. The school offered a college preparatory curriculum, night and summer classes, and encouraged the enrollment of international students. Rhodes graduates include actors James Caan and Robert DeNiro.

To avoid those boring kids, John had quit school at sixteen after our first move to Westchester, New York. He'd screwed the girls, had the buddies, and come in from Jersey on Saturday afternoons to jam at the Paramount Theater and sit through four shows of road movies in order to stomp with Benny Goodman on the stage in between. But to hell with saddle shoes and bobbed hair and football games and proms and yearbooks. He had thrown it all over at sixteen to write poetry in his half-basement room in our home in Chappaqua and flirt with my fifth grade teacher. He came on with her—a lot of Byron, Shelley and Keats, narrowed sexy stares, his blond hair in a high wave to the back and a pipe between his teeth. She came to the house often, giggled and fluttered in the living room under his stare—he was sixteen and a sex killer already—and one afternoon she screeched out, "Oh, Byron, Shelley and Keats, that trio of musical treats!" Then she went downstairs to his den to read his poems.

John, who never did graduate from high school, later worked at the *Reader's Digest* in Mt. Kisco, New York, met Marian Miliambro from the Italian end of town, was drafted into the Navy, and after boot camp, married Marian and was sent to San Diego where we all followed to live with my aunt in Altadena. But that was another coast, another story, and over now. By January 1947, he was taking graduate courses at Columbia, writing, and meeting crazy people.

He realized that I hadn't been much of a success at all-American Horace Greeley High School in Chappaqua—with my stringy hair, my braces, my flat chest, I was no winner, although I did play a mean game of hockey. John was impatient. "Look up—what's the matter? You never liked kids your own age anyway. So now there's older guys. You'll have the best experience of your life. Go!"

John was right. *He* had switched to the older ones: Marian herself was three years older—a working girl. Maybe skinny Liz with the pout, seven years younger, should switch too—to the vets in the new private school and the girls dolled up to look eighteen. Liz had soulful eyes, fetching in their green, retreating way. Plus, I reasoned, there'd be guys, unlike the public neighborhood school, Julia Richmond High

School, that I would otherwise have attended, since at that time, all the public schools in New York were segregated—and my local one was just girls, girls, girls.

So go I did, and soon I had settled into a strange urban brand of happiness. I fixed up my little room—hung and folded my few clothes, straightened my desk-table and lined up my 78s in albums of twelve pockets in a low shelf that held my turntable—now a portable with a cover and a speaker—next to the army cot I slept on. In front of the window, which looked over the back building to a huge apartment house, I could see an older man with a mustache reading his paper and sometimes he'd go into his bathroom where, through the small window, I would watch him masturbate as I listened to Illinois Jacquet at Jazz at the Philharmonic.

My new high school was housed in an old brownstone with small classrooms tucked in corners and a curving staircase with a heavy banister; the older guys, big, swearing, sexy talkers, tender-hearted, gallant, ironic with me; the pancaked girls in furs; our geometry teacher, a large pleasant man, drunk after lunch and stumbling in high spirits through our geometry class. There was little to do in that brownstone but drink of the fountain and eat of the tree.

The vets got on well with the teachers, who were mostly older vets themselves. In each class, they immediately formed a bond, and we girls had to keep up to the mark. The guys wanted to work hard and soak up a year of everything in half a year. French, algebra, biology, English (four years in two), world history, American history—racing on and on through semester after semester—a frog one day, a parallelogram the next, the *passé simple* a week later. Book reports every other week and no Bret Harte stuff. The big boys—Dostoyevsky, Melville, Balzac—clearly put more gleam in Mr. Perry's eyes, and the denser our take on them, the more As on our papers. If we fastened onto a side drama—"a little lower layer," as he used to call it, and proved in an obscure, excitable tirade how it could change our lives forever, Mr. Perry might even scrawl a red, excitable paragraph of his own under the A.

The guys and the teachers worked each other over, and the class-room bar was raised higher and higher. The girls in their pancake make-up and furs had to jump pretty high to keep up, a bad bargain for some who thought they wanted to seduce the big guys and get by on red lips and eye shadow but found they had to do advanced algebra in a couple of months and read *Madame Bovary* in French 3 in a week. They heaved and panted and mostly did keep up. They were smart girls, the daughters of dentists and lawyers, but it was hard for a sixteen-year-old, even with fancy hair and a show-off bust, to snare guys in their twenties just back from the skillful, melancholy beds of French and German women. I had a special girlfriend, Margaret, who was dumpy with bleached blond hair, scarlet lips, and blood red killer nails. She dressed in furs and, yes, she was the daughter of a dentist. The two of us would smoke and talk about the guys and the lore they were feeding us and all the things we'd like to do with them. It was a wild and racy intellectualism that pulled us along through Rhodes School, where between classes we all smoked against the high gray fence across the street, bantering and flirting against the back wall of the sculpture garden at the Museum of Modern Art.

At lunchtime everybody would break through the front door and run down the block to a favorite bar on Sixth Avenue. Booths filled up with guys and maybe one lucky girl to perk up the scenery—hamburg-ers, grilled cheese and glasses of beer all around, the girl often coming in under the guys' cover. Except for me. Oh I wore lipstick, but my hair—brown and dropping lifeless on my shoulders (which were round, by the way, because I was too tall, five feet eight, to be comfortable) stumped me. I hated it. It never *did* anything, like stay under a kerchief or a clip, curl at the ends, wave at the top. It was lazy and messy and never got its act together. So I hated it and left it alone and let it go its lousy, unco-operative way. I didn't wash it much—the bathtub was the cockroaches' special apartment house, neither my mother nor I used it much. I didn't wear bras, nothing yet to put in them. And I had pimples—bad ones that on bad days were swollen polka dots on my cheeks. I wore braces like silver armor on my teeth, which required tuning up every three weeks. My orthodontist was on Fifth Avenue and Seventy-fifth Street, and a daughter of his could have been a fur-clad classmate of mine.

But I wasn't such a total dog as you might think. There's a picture of me on the roof of 681 holding my kitty in my lap. I have a straight knee-length skirt and a blazer over a light blouse with wide lapels lying over the collar. My hair is combed so that it bobs together at the shoulders and my eyes, which were soft and pretty, are bent towards Kitty—very tender. My knees are angled together and the long calves in their stockings are shapely enough to touch. Really nice legs—a plus, not to be slighted. The lips are set in a closed love-smile at Kitty. You can't see the pock-marked skin or the armored teeth or the nothing breasts. No, anyone would say—a pretty girl with a tender heart and a sexy pair of gams.

The big school guys saw it all—good and bad—but they didn't seem to care and took it all for what it was. I laughed a lot and loved them for kidding me and telling me their life tales. Granted, they cleaned up the sex-stories, but always gave me the revisions, and they joked and kibitzed among themselves for my benefit. I laughed too, as though I *dug* (the verb of the day on New York streets) everything they said and left unsaid as well. They flirted a little with the dolls—not too much and no follow through as far as I could tell—but they *liked* me. One very tall fellow (but they were all tall), full-bodied with a handsome (but they were all handsome) wavy head of hair, walked beside me every three weeks on the hexagonal stones by Central Park up to my dentist—joshing about the date he was going to have for the night and asking me if I liked any of the six teenage boys in the school, if I was ready for our geometry test the next day, and if I'd noticed how drunk our teacher had been after lunch today.

I didn't have a clue about working up my sexual assets. I was lazy. Twirling strings of hair into pin curls was nonsensical and useless in my case. I went through jars of Stridex, which made no headway against the mini-volcanoes on my face. I was exasperated, bored and finally scornful of my crummy attributes in the "girl" department. Consequently, I was set free to learn. And so I did—beginning a course of learning and yearning. While living in a world of big brothers, especially my brother John, I stopped fooling around and listened. Listening and desiring.

Learning isn't worth a fig if it isn't driven by desire. I wanted these guys. They knew stuff about life—how it was done, the language of people—big people who could hurt and love and kill just like the people Dostoyevsky and Balzac wrote about. In this city of big brothers, learning was now thrilling because it made you love. All teachers worth their salt are yearned after in the flesh by their best students. I was a good student in high school, getting almost straight As and in love every day of the year. Sometimes falling in love two and three times a day. On any given day—let's say, Friday—I would set aside a few minutes after class to fake a question of my economics teacher with whom I had been deeply in love all year. Then Margaret and I would have a cigarette by the MoMA fence with Tom Grady—a dark-haired perfect beauty of a vet who we both wanted to undress so we could explore his hidden beauties. We'd walk him to Grand Central Station, and when he looked at me, I died and laughed to steady the Chesterfield in my shaking hand. At five o'clock, I would drag my mother down to the bookstore on Forty-second Street where Paul Salomon, a tall brilliant fellow who got even more As than I did, worked after school. Paul, whose soul (and body too) I longed to capture in my hopeless hands at least once a week. Oh, the bitter dead end of Friday afternoon! To be in love three times—mind-teacher, body-teacher, and Paul the soul-teacher—and at the door of a loveless, desolate weekend.

Learn, desire, love. Even in my primitive teenage brain, I feared that fulfillment of any one of these desires would cancel out the others—typical teenage paralysis. And at least for that year I stayed clean and didn't push the issue. I didn't know how anyway, as I said before. Besides, I was getting my own private compensation—all the legends, all the facts, all the different flavors of life, which were enough for a time. Soon, though, need would begin pushing me to deal with my own sexuality. I remember petting to climax with one of the young non-vets in school, and a black pal—a vet—willingly took me to bed in the name of friendship.

But first there was my big-brother world. The weekend might have been desolate of love, but the real big brother, John, could fill any weekend full enough with his talk. And I was probably most in love with him.

Chapter 2

John

———— By the time we settled into our new home in 5D, John had seriously committed himself to writing. He was twenty-one, married, going to Columbia to get the GI Bill money and bent fervidly to his vocation. From my upstairs vantage point, I could see that his entire life was being sucked up by the effort to make his place in literature. Wife worked to support it, Mom pitched in on the rent and bought many family dinners at Joe's Restaurant on Third Avenue. Whole libraries from Fourth-Avenue used bookstores had to be hoarded, bookshelves covering the walls from floor-to-ceiling had to be tacked together, hundreds of beers had to be drunk, and days had to be free for feverish thought and spurts on the typewriter—time reserved for reading those walls of books and later grabbing onto writers, jazz, and all those people who never feared the night—the dopesters, jailbirds, wild bar men, girls who every night rushed into the dark, certain that it would finally give up its last drop of truth.

All of New York was a little crazy like that in 1947 and '48. After all, we weren't Paris and London, Berlin and Rome—bombed-out in body and spirit. No, New York in the postwar forties felt like it was rising up, up, a mighty phoenix free from the fear of death that threatened to clip its wings. Painters left Europe to settle in the

Cedar Tavern in Greenwich Village, new jazz musicians left their regional bands and cities to surface on Fifty-second Street and Broadway and at Minton's. Young writers shouted epiphanies to each other on MacDougal Street and at P.J. Clarke's and Glennon's bars on Third Avenue and Fifty-fourth Street. If most of the world was surely dead—and World War II was the greatest killer in history—where on earth could the last shoot of creativity break ground? The United Nations had landed in New York, a world-class city with all its buildings still intact, but more crucial were the sprouts of creative genius that broke through its fertile soil. Goddamn, were we lucky to be there! New York was big, dark, motley, and cheap enough to furnish the messy subsoil of hipsters, cafeteria criminals, hanger-ons, bop fanatics, and petty bohemians that it takes to seed the geniuses of art.

John, on many solitary afternoons, must have felt the ground breaking under him—geological plates of belief and tradition shifting into new, powerful, maybe even terrifying gear. The roar of the traffic below on Lexington Avenue must have seemed the rumble of a cataclysm that would clear our ruined decks and set us the task of building a new life from scratch. He was quietly frantic to join the fertile mayhem—the signs of life rising only *here* in a mostly dead planet. I know he was excited to distraction because he *talked* to me about it, either in his own apartment or upstairs in ours.

John was thin with the slightly starved look of the fanatic intellectual. But his straight blond hair combed back and his lean cheeks gave him a perpetually boyish air. At first he read poetry, mostly W. B. Yeats. We were living in that world falling apart, looking for the center inside all the anarchy. He would read in a doomsday voice, puffing Chesterfields at the line breaks, the heavy thoughts bearing down at the end: ". . . slouches toward Bethlehem to be born," ". . . foul rag and bone shop of the heart." He'd stop at the end and glare and gleam across to me. I was filled with fear and awe and I was silent like a stone. If he were impatient, he'd prod me. "Well, what do you think, Liz? Say something!" "It's great!" I'd turn my hands up—confused, helpless, without a voice, awed as much by John as by Yeats, but clearly a learning lover of words. To his credit, he never gave up on me, though I felt and acted brainless, close-mouthed, and even pouty at times.

Who cared? He needed a pupil, a listener, an acolyte whose silence confirmed his voice and its discoveries. "Look at the list on the inside cover of the Modern Library books. Get them, all of them, or borrow mine. Read, read!" he demanded. So I began checking off the ones he stressed. There was a lot of Dostoyevsky—he said that we were living in "Dusty's" world—here, now. New York in 1947 and '48 was St. Petersburg in the 1870s. He'd read whole speeches of Melville's Ahab and urged the whole of that slow, magnificent *Moby Dick* on me: "Back in 1855 Melville *knew* the dark side of the world—our world. Amazing! Right here—New York! Read 'Bartleby, the Scrivener.' You've read *Hamlet*. Now read *Pierre*—Melville's great tragedy of New York, our own New York! And he's buried in Woodlawn Cemetery in the Bronx. Can you believe it! It's all happening here, now! The little lower layer is all around us!"

He sent me swooning with Thomas Wolfe, in all the gush of "lost-ness" until I would chant aloud in my room, "Oh lost, and by the wind-grieved ghost, come back again!" moaning in Manhattan with Eugene Gant over the loss of his brother Ben in North Carolina. After all, John said that Wolfe had lived alone in Brooklyn and walked over that iconic bridge night after night. There was also a great deal of D. H. Lawrence. *He*, John said, was the prophet of now and of the future too. He bestowed visions of the flesh and sex holiness that would rise out of our modern ruins. "A new human nature, a truly new world," John lectured to me. "Read him—all of them—then finally *The Plumed Serpent*! The direction of the new world between men and women. Read him, Liz! My new friends and I see the signs all around." Then he might look a little fiercely at me—gauging my readiness. I was only fourteen, after all. "He delivers the message. Sex is the deepest experience in life!" Then he'd soften the message for my age: "You'll learn all that later."

Often I would go downstairs to his place, 4C, to study music. "We're through with Dixieland, Liz, those days of simple codas—trumpet with the tune, clarinet high, trombone low, drum steady—quick solos never far from the song—and those all-outs, the coda all over again, only louder and *short*. Not enough to it. The new guys call it moldy fig jazz. In fact, we don't use the word 'jazz' anymore. No, the new stuff is BOP, Liz, Bebop—and it's wild, it breaks all the rules, and it's *complex*. You have to really listen to the inside of it. Now *listen!*"

He would play Charlie Parker's *Ornithology*, and I would do what
I was told, always eager to learn John's lessons. I listened by looking right at the turntable, as he did, hoping to catch the secret from
the needle's path across the 78 turning there. Listening and looking
and not hearing yet—the sax too high and fast to follow, the few
instruments playing the coda together, the coda itself, a series of
jerky phrases stopping everywhere—in the beginning, the middle of
a phrase—and the drum that you couldn't tap your foot to. Then I
watched John moving his head forwards and back with his neck to
get himself inside the crazy rhythm. When it was over, he gleamed
and shouted, "Listen, Liz!" and he hummed that old tune, "How
High the Moon" that I knew every note of. I didn't get it. "Now
listen again, *hard!*" He placed the needle at the beginning of the
record. He hummed loud with the coda—Bird and Miles, and John
humming "How High the Moon" along with them. They angled
into and out of each other, meeting at the right places—the melo-
dies echoing sweetly and ending on the same note—and the world
came together. It began.

I followed bop right behind John. It wasn't easy, and he had to
coach me with easier stuff (Jazz at the Philharmonic—Flip Phillips, Illinois Jacquet and the Honkers) until I was ready for Dexter Gordon and Wardell Gray on "The Hunt." Roy Eldridge until
Dizzy Gillespie, George Shearing a long time until Lennie Tristano,
Art Tatum to Bud Powell. Thelonius Monk's "'Round Midnight,"
strange notes on sad, singable mood-tune. I had to get used to saxes
everywhere. Before, there'd only been mellow Bud Freeman; next,
the mellow and more complex Coleman Hawkins; until at last Lester Young ("Prez") and the pure bell tone that spoke of a weird and
beautiful cosmic loneliness, the voice now of all the new saxes in
New York including that of Charlie "Bird" Parker. It took me a year
to really *hear* Parker's "little lower layer," but when I finally did, I felt
as if I had reached the end of jazz and I could stay there forever.

I would go to small cramped record shops along Sixth Avenue and
buy bop records at discounts every week, playing them over and over
by my bed at night, learning all the solos, until I could whistle Dizzy

cavorting from the top, Charlie weaving too fast to see, Bud Powell's mad cascading runs on "Tea For Two," and the beauty of Bird on "Warmin' Up a Riff" with Dizzy on piano laughing at him. I whistled them all, moving my head from the neck, forward first, then back.

But John, bless his bulldozing heart, didn't stop with the first team. After all, living where I did, going to school with a fair number of jazz lovers and only a few blocks from two great jazz venues, Fifty-second Street and the upper half of Times Square along Broadway, I would have bumped up against the Dizzys, Parkers, Lester Youngs, Monks, and Roaches somewhere along the way. But thorough John insinuated a second string.

To point up this phase of my education with John, I'm going to borrow from baseball, a sport that John paid no attention to but that I became fanatic about, hauling friend Margaret every other week in 1948 to Ebbets Field while she dragged me alternate weeks to Yankee Stadium—neither of us went kicking or screaming either. When there were no Dodgers or Yankees available, we'd subway up to the Polo Grounds, where I would sit in the right field stands thinking how I had never seen anything so casually graceful as Tommy Holmes of the Boston Braves walking slowly around with head down in the perpetual baseball meditation between plays. Like New York City, I was in love with baseball and everybody who played it. Oh, the enchantment of baseball where the action time is no more than a quarter of the two-hour-plus game, where the major entertainment for me became the study of meditation: the strolling at position, the occasional toss and catch, the scuffing the grass, leaning on a hip, the head down or turning nowhere, the expression impassive, inward. At the ballpark, I learned the beauties of stop and pause and the grace of doing nothing. Yes, so I listed the teams in my room—all the players in both leagues—and I tried in one season to see them all and to learn the rhythm of their gestures in the nothingness of baseball time. I probably saw most of them in the late forties. But John would have none of that. The music of baseball was too slow for him at that time, so I kept my baseball nuttiness to myself.

But in his own way, he came along and filled my jazz bench with second-stringers, artists that to this day I listen to. There was Howard McGhee, with his clear forceful drive on trumpet, and scores of tenor sax men like Lucky Thompson, and everybody's secret tenor hero, Wardell Gray, quietly driving Dexter Gordon to desperate squawks on "The Hunt" and "The Chase." And all the wonderful back-up pianists keeping the chord changes a flawless ladder of song for the soloists to climb—Duke Jordan, Dodo Marmarosa, and Al Haig. The crazy new drummers that you couldn't tap a foot to, instead learning to jerk your head at odd stresses and letting out erratic "pows"— Kenny Clarke, Don Lamond, and Roy Haynes. The second team John instructed me in was often more accessible, and more than that, it filled out a world and made bebop a huge extended family, the smallest members of which sustained the giants. Because of John, I know them, and unless I lose my mental way in decline, I will carry their names to my grave.

As John reported back to me on art and life in our city and in our time, I listened, learned and *became*. You see, the war had changed everything. This was an "existential" world, turning upside down in W. H. Auden's "Age of Anxiety." The rules were gone, but we weren't mourning their loss like the lost generation of the twenties. No, John said, "We're raging into extremes, or we're looking for a new way. The last thing we are is cynical." He'd pour these ideas into my mother on many evenings, side-glancing at me, hating the way our mother was trying to find her way in this world—all her Unity Day-books and Vedanta[6] and the soft brand of Irish mystical poetry she loved. His voice was strident, impatient, angry, always side-glancing at me, shooting darts through my sulks. I was speechless—across the room pouting in wonder and fear at all the tales of the new life and the terrifying conclusions it led him to.

---

6. Editor's Note: Unity Day books are spiritual books published by the Unity School of Christianity, a religious movement founded by Charles and Myrtle Fillmore in 1889. According to the Unity website, the not-for-profit organization is based on the teachings of Jesus and the healing power of prayer. Vedanta is one of the world's most ancient religious philosophies and is based on the Vedas, the sacred scriptures of India. It is the philosophical foundation of Hinduism.

When visiting upstairs in 5D, John was often on a shock trip, as if he wanted to hurl me and our mother into wild and scary recognitions. His tales of a burgeoning Beat generation spat bullets at us. "Last night Alan Harrington and Edward Stringham took us down to the maddest party in New York! A horrible, filthy apartment in Chelsea filled with subterranean guys and girls who care for nothing but booze and tea and all extremes of experience. A girl took off her clothes and danced to the loudest record player on the block. She spread her legs . . . What's a matter, Mom, don't turn away—this is life in our time!" She would look in my direction. "Don't you think . . . ?"

"Oh, Mom," John would counter, "Liz can take it. She's fifteen and she's going to see a lot before too long. She might as well hear it from me. So anyway, this girl is standing wide open in front of some dark Dostoyevskean theology student I've seen at Allen's (Ginsberg), a guy named Russell Durgin. He's in the corner brooding, and then, what's got to be the wildest man in New York leaps in between them and throws the girl on the floor and starts making her right in front of Durgin, yelling above the crowd, 'I only do this to show you, dear Russell, that God doesn't exist, that he's left town for greener pastures—and has left me, yes, *me*, Bill Cannastra, in charge!' He screwed her there for all to see, gulping whiskey all the while. But no one paid any attention! No one cared! They were all pursuing their own insanities, lurching, petting, passing sticks of tea—bottles and glasses strewn and broken, and lighted butts catching discarded clothes on fire and people shouting revelations across the wreckage of the rooms. People knocked on the door—neighbors, police. Nobody heard.

"Finally, this wild demon, Cannastra, led everybody out, even the naked girl, and down the block in a crazy conga line and into a longshoremen's bar and went up to a drunken merchant marine, shouting, 'Give me a big wet kiss.' He grabbed the guy around the neck and kissed him full and hard on the mouth, 'Just to show you, darling, how to break down all the doors!' The guy was astounded, like he'd seen the devil himself and couldn't move. Cannastra affects everyone this way—the authorities, the law—and they leave him alone, so that he runs mad and raging and free through the city on some private mission of damnation—and everybody's afraid to touch him. With a bottle swinging in his hand, Cannastra led us all on a lurching dance out the door. Alan took us home and explained, 'You see, Bill was an old classmate of ours at Harvard. Perhaps he's gone nuts. But there's method to it. Russell Durgin has pined away in love-lament for that girl for a year and Bill only makes out with her in front of him at his parties 'To show Durgin' he says, 'that such love is the fast way to hell.' He's convinced, of course, that that's where we're living—right now—1948, right here, New York City—Hell!'"

John puts out his cigarette, stuffs the pack in his shirt pocket, and gets up. "Got to get down to work, to Marian." He is irritated, finding us hopeless and mad at himself for bothering. He leaves. I'm trembling in my middle and go into my little room where I play some gentle George Shearing to ease my way into the night of this awful, thrilling new world that John is shoving down my throat.

John was severe like that much of the time. It seemed as if he wanted to wound, even kill us with dark knowledge. The severe times seemed to occur when our mother was present. She seemed to drive him to the limits of hell fire. Her stubborn, melancholy trust in the god of love enraged him. He'd come in the door, sit in the wing chair, take out the cigarettes, and ask through tight lips, "Are you still playing for that Unity place?" Mom did play piano at meetings of The Unity School of Christianity. "Yes, they do need me, and yes, I do like the quiet simple atmosphere there." She'd lay down this timid gauntlet, and he'd snicker, gear up for battle, and start firing his cannons. Smoke would come out of his mouth with a scornful laugh. "It's pretty to think so, Mom. What about the war we've been through and the bomb that's waiting to blow this island apart any minute—and the rules that are all gone and the chaos of life in our time? It's almost *criminal* to turn away and hide in the soppy words of the *Daily Word*." And so it went.

But often he came in flush and beside himself with excitement. 5D wasn't so bad, after all, a little room with a huge skylight where all life would stop for him, mother and sister sitting in wait—for what? My mother probably wanted love and filial respect, warm tolerance, if not understanding. I craved brotherly affection. I didn't get much—whatever that is, at fifteen I didn't know that most affection comes unbidden. What I got was much better—the inside dope on a new way of life, along with some handy ideas to deal with it and a lot of the literature and philosophy from the past that had prophesied its coming. "Dusty, Melville, Kierkegaard, Blake. They all saw our world coming. Yeats and Lawrence wrote perfect visions of our own post-World-War-II life, life without God, facing the end every day," as John would say.

I did worry my head off about that bomb—living in the bull's eye of destruction, Fifty-sixth and Lexington Avenue, on the island of Manhattan, all of us running around to schools and jobs and cafeterias and bars, smoking and laughing and eager for everything, all the everything that might end this afternoon in the middle of a beer, a geometry class, coffee in the Waldorf Cafeteria on Sixth Avenue, Wardell Gray cutting into Dexter on record one of "The Hunt," a Dean Acheson speech at a Soviet-American friendship rally—and goddamn America with that Iron Curtain and Truman Doctrine, always needling and provoking the end of it all—until my cot and the turntable always going 'round and 'round with the Bird flying out of it is the tiniest sigh of air in the millionth particle of ash that adds its dot of black to all the other dots of the planet—the little rooms with record players stilled into sighs of air—and the cloud of earth grays, pales, and becomes the faint dying sigh of the cosmos. Yes, John had something there with all his doom and mayhem talk—the bomb hanging there in the bluest sky forever.

"So each man makes his life day by day, playing life by ear. What we all feel now is that all there is *is experience*—get it all, every bit to the outer limits—like Cannastra even. The other night he climbed up the girder of the El and swayed above the street laughing like a maniac and proclaiming that he saw the promised land, looking west to Broadway maybe, and that it was Hell, 'Yes, ladies and gentlemen, Hell! And flowing with milk and honey!' Everybody stood transfixed! Anyway, all the wise ones have told us over and over till now we *know* it in our bones—the body's the only way to the spirit."

Mom tuned him out. I tuned him in, cringing on the couch, appalled, but thrilled, each nerve end a receptor. Of course, he talked about books and school, such as the words of Susanne Langer in one of her philosophy classes that he was taking. I can't remember exactly, except that John seemed to argue with her, and she treated this stringy youth in horn rims as an equal. He also mentioned the Collums, Padraic and Mary, reading Yeats and entrancing the class.

John never bothered much with small things—the silly tastes of a fifteen-year-old girl. So I kept a private life of trivia from him—Margaret and I smoking and giggling in the entrance to 681 about boys and cars, my clinging to bad and moldy jazz (early ragtime James P. Johnson, sentimental Erroll Garner), compiling great lists of all the baseball players on all the teams and vowing to see them all in one summer, with the "kids" left in the school, shouting out lyrics to thirties musicals on the steps of St. Thomas Church on the corner of Fifty-third and Fifth Avenue. John was twenty-two and heavy with the first onset of gravity. Music was complex and new, books were prophetic, people were geniuses or visionaries or demons, parties were revelations, sex was deep and monumental, New York was the world-city that would lead the way to the decline of the West. (They talked all the time about Oswald Spengler and his monumental two-volume treatise *Decline of the West.*) John's world. It was riotous—filled with laughter and noise, alive with flailing arms and maniacal screeches. I was a witness and sat shrunken in a corner at some gatherings. But all of it was weighted with exhilarating meaning. Every note, every word, every gesture would change their lives forever. Next to that, most of my life was paltry. I was a moth darting around the light.

But when he was alone with me—usually on afternoons when my mother was at work and I was home from school—John was genial and even inquisitive, asking me about books and the records I was buying—questions to prod me to question him, which I wanted to do. He was usually so friendly in these sessions, and he wanted to talk—tales and lessons again, but with a happy voice now, pleased that I was such a really good learner. And I *was* then—eager, not scared, learning finally to "dig." That was the word, that was the

way, that was the heart with which to greet life. Open the mind
and heart to everything without any baggage. "You *dig*, Liz, take it
from the boppers." I'd nod, maybe smile and say "Great!" to some
tale, some notion, and I'd know I "dug." I'd get elated after these
sessions and play Parker or Thelonius Monk and it would make
some new sense that told me I was on the threshold of revelations
that would change my life and maybe the world's too. Exhilarated,
lesson learned, enlightened. Yes, John taught me to bring nothing to
the table, to put up no barriers, to be blank and fearless, and to learn.

It was all the new people he was meeting that fueled John's enthusiasm and vision. He gave me long, colorful introductions to them,
especially the men. He could talk forever to me because my as-yet-
unlived life would gladly stop at any time for him. Maybe he was prac-
ticing his craft, working up descriptive skills in these introductions.

Alan Harrington was probably the first. I think John had met
him in 1947 through the painter who lived across the street from
them on Eighty-ninth Street, Alan Wood-Thomas, and his wife,
Annabelle. Alan Harrington was tall, six feet four or so with short
legs and a waist that twisted and fell to his knees. His shirts were
always detached from his pants, his hair was a dirty blond crew
cut, one of his eyes shot off to the wall, and a hand was always
groping inside his belt, maybe in a futile search for those shirttails. John probably went into details; he was known to do so, after
all. Anyway, Alan intrigued him. Such quick brilliance and quietly
bossy wit murmured through a half-smile of thin, sentient lips, and
he was a writer too, working on a novel about Hal Hingham and
Merko, the human fly.

He had ideas too—some doctrine of centralism that was crucial
to the sea of advertising that America was beginning to drown in.
Something about how we were all losing ourselves to hucksters
who insinuated themselves into all of us until we begged for their
wares, their ideas, their feelings. John was fascinated by this tall Harvard fellow, who had a quiet come-on with women and who was
married to a lovely, perhaps silly but sweet lady, Virginia. I soon saw,
after I knew him a while, that Alan was hopelessly enchanted by

Wood-Thomas's pre-pubescent daughter, Leanne. The fascination
continued for years after his divorce and long relationship with a
Russian émigré named Marya and after we had all left the city. The
tall man with starry eyes—even the wall-eyed one—angling his long
torso over the pretty ballet teenager—my Humbert Humbert[7] in the
flesh. Of course, I detested him, with all the jealous vitriol of an older
girl who didn't have the physical goods and was always stunned into
silence by brilliance—listening all those hours to a brother sage of
Manhattan—and who would come to see all the girls of "the men"
as rivals. But Alan was the key, after all—the first star who introduced
John to the entire crowd that would make a real writer of him, that
would open up seasons of revelations that would soon spin off to me
upstairs in my room with the record player.

John also talked to me about the rest of Alan's Harvard crowd,
for instance Edward Stringham, a lovely sensitive blond fellow
who was a homosexual and lived up by Columbia and loved classical music. He was handsome and kind and smiled epiphanies to
me about the exaltation of buying a new record and putting off
the joy of it until after hours of chores and friends so that by the
time you lie down to sleep you are almost orgiastic in anticipation
of the morning when, with trembling hand, you'll put the needle
on the disc. There was also Roger Lyndon, another Harvard man,
who was teaching math at Princeton. John described him as a
simple man who couldn't talk to anybody about his business and
so all he did was drink and laugh and dance wildly and crash into
things. And finally there was Bill Cannastra, the arch demon whom
I never saw but who haunted a corner of my thoughts for several
years, all the stories about him and his disturbing demise.

Sometime later in 1948, John, through Alan Harrington, went to
a party where he met Jack Kerouac and Allen Ginsberg, both part of
the Columbia gang and both shorter, marginal, wilder, and darker.
They were always accompanied by the specter of Lucien Carr, also

---

7. Editor's Note: Humbert Humbert, a middle-aged man obsessed with pre-pubescent girls, is
the main character in and narrator of Vladimir Nabokov's novel *Lolita* (1955).

from Columbia—young, blond, and a murderer. John called Lucien the most beautiful boy in the world: "Stalked by a maniacal, obsessive older man all the way from the Midwest, who sought total possession, until one night in Riverside Park, he pleaded and accosted him and Lucien stabbed him and threw him in the river. He got off on self-defense. He's another wild and crazy youth who shouts outrageous things from the top of his head—and they all meet in the Greenwich Village pad of William (Bill) S. Burroughs, an older guy from a patrician family—the Burroughs Adding Machine people. They all get stoned on drugs and formulate ecstatic theories of aesthetics. Of course, I've heard from Harrington about this Kerouac football player from Columbia who's writing this mammoth novel that's being passed around the city in a bag. He was there at the party—dark, shy, brooding—stocky and strong looking—natural athlete, natural writer—the perfect natural."

In the summer of '48, when I was in summer school and eyeing a dark heavy-set vet by the fence who stood alone some way off with his own cigarette, sunk in private study, remote and inaccessible beyond a half-smile in my direction, my fantasy lover of the season, John was cementing his relationships with these ex-Columbia inspirational madmen. He was clearly entranced in his own summer infatuation with them, as I was to hear many afternoons under the open skylight with the hot soot dropping silently around us. These and other strange newcomers occupied his attention, making him excited, agitated, and they clearly undermined the novel he was trying to write. It was a book he had talked about before—about a hired killer named Frankel who suffers Dostoyevskean angst. I had written a book report on *Crime and Punishment*, and thought that John's novel must be something along those lines. He hadn't said too much about it, though, and it seemed to frustrate and irritate him until I thought that writing a novel must be a job too stupendous for mortals to tackle. My father thought writing was stupid play work, a pose for living it up, an excuse for wild booze parties. But it was John who taught me that it was the hardest work in the world. All these astounding underground people he was meeting would force a break with the Frankel saga that was driving the spirit out of him. And they would later lead him to write the first real novel that was in him.

Before that, though, a detour emerged in the form of a person who would set John on a marginal but fruitful course. He became connected with Jay Landesman, who created and published the avant garde Beat journal *Neurotica*, and through Landesman met Gershon Legman, a dark fat man who lived with his wife and cats in a little cottage in the Bronx. Of course, I pictured it as Poe's cottage on the Grand Concourse. John said it wasn't far from there. It was filled with mountains of books, comic books, and other piles of print media—his research material for some gigantic encyclopedic polemic about sex and violence in America. Legman was a fanatic, a dogmatic, a demagogue, and the most brilliant and subversive scholar of sex and violence in American culture, too far-out, on-target, and paranoid to ever be heard. John was mesmerized by the powerful fat man of the Bronx and brought him to 5D one early evening to impress us. He was arrogant about his new icon and about his own position as a true acolyte.

Gershon was fat, but tightly knit together. I think his black hair was full and wavy and parted half-heartedly in the middle. A round face and serious black eyes with a hint of anger in them that made them live. He was aggressive and alert and didn't small talk. Focused on his obsession. But I liked him; he didn't frighten me, even though John had painted him so fiercely. But it seemed he could find his obsessions anywhere—so he was not easily bored, even in our drab, neat little room. All his surroundings confirmed his research and conclusion—sex, with violence murdering and displacing it everywhere. We had a tabby cat, Kitty, housebound and un-spayed. It was hot, and she was in heat and she yowled and raised her backend up in all our faces as she prowled in and out of the room toward the locked door. My fastidious mother apologized for her. But Gershon was quiet, watching her intently. "No, no, no. Of course, it is a crime to take the sex out of pets. I assume she doesn't go out. But still the sex is in her and at least she can express the longing. I'm glad and I commend you for letting her live. You haven't committed violence on her. A small sign in a culture that is violating and neutering the live sex out of us in a bloodbath of media mayhem." In *Nothing More to Declare* my brother recalls the opposite story, that Gershon was angry because Kitty had been spayed, but I lived with her for six years and she was in heat regularly throughout every year. That was my one encounter with Gershon Legman—an outsider, even of outsiders. Where John's other friends formed groups of light in what they thought of as a black world, Gershon was a single laser beam of blare directed smack at our innards. He was a good lone raider who I hear ended up in the south of France, having written his monumental work, *Love and Death*, and fought the good fight, a whole man, living at home with himself in France. I was impressed, and I still think of him as the pure knight rescuing an Eros besieged to this day from all sides. It all fit, you see, with all John's talk about D.H. Lawrence and the sexual body freeing itself from the bonds of the world, all the rules and mayhem and murder, to lead us to the spirit. It was an exhilarating, frustrating, and bitter learning for a fifteen-year-old who couldn't yet start on the sex journey that was the obsession of everybody in those days.

Chapter 3

Jack Kerouac and Company

——— I don't remember the first time I met Jack Kerouac. That is strange because I loved him right off, even if I can't pinpoint when the "right off" was. I see him sitting in a straight chair in John's apartment. It's afternoon. The chair is between a low bookcase by the couch and the kitchen table. I am on another couch, which forms a right angle with more couch, both with bookcases filling the walls above them. Across from me is the kitchen area—apartment fridge with hot plate and shelves. The phonograph is across from the couch near Jack, and, of course, a loud record is playing, this one a mambo. John has been talking mambo to me and urging me to listen to Perez Prado—which, of course, I have done and now have a growing twelve-pocket album of Prado, Puente, Pupi Campo, Tito Rodriguez, Machito, and Dizzy. Jack has a saucepan upside down between his legs with the handle in his crotch and he is bongo-ing. He bobs his head a bit and looks around—at the music, at John bouncing near the player, at me. A lick of black hair falls to his forehead, his wide, fragile lips pucker out and then break into a smile, the eyes light up. They are sentient and intimate in a four-o'clock-shadowed face. Oh, yes, Jack's eyes in those hot forties days—full of youth, vulnerable, asking for love and pain. Of course, I loved him, having heard all about him—the genius writer, the shy manner devoid of wit and repartee—then seeing him and feeling that sensual kindness for all earth's creatures—even me, awkward with incipient sex, filled with too much knowledge to know what to do with, and unable to voice anything more than "That's great! Yes! Really?" and then pout in frustration. Jack was gentle and patient with me, the way he would be with other lost but believing creatures. I loved him and would continue to in the background of my life for the next few years. Later my mother gave me a copy of *Big Sur* for my birthday, "In memory of dear Jack," she said. She called him "Sweet Jack" and never minded my being alone with him in 5D when she had to be away at work.

So Jack was there in the chair and I don't know when he first appeared. For a few months of that year I see him there, multiplied in my fancy to numberless times. I can't trust this fancy. It may have been three or four, it may have been fifteen. He appeared there one afternoon and later metamorphosed into a presence—his double taps on the pan (he tried to teach me the simple mambo alternating two-beats), the quick wave with the cigarette ("I'm a Phillip Morris man. You like Chesterfields, Liz, like your brother?"), the puckered wide lips opening in the fluid smile, the quiet manner, always paying attention, laughing and nodding with care at my monosyllabic responses—("Great record, John!" "Yes, Liz, you're right! You already dig the good stuff."), the weird sincerity of heart that informed his face, hands, thick torso, even the blue canvas shoes with the crepe soles tapping on the floor. What could I do? He was the Holy Grail for a withdrawn, romantic girl. In those years, the years of knowing Jack, I never saw the demonic boozer, the guy who loved and left, the nasty Jack who flared up in paranoid rages with many who loved and revered him, my brother John for one. Jack came very close to me at times, and I was to be hurt in my unsung heart by the final distance he could only feel for such an unformed adolescent soul— on her way but not yet there, was probably his feeling at the time.

But Jack took me seriously, and he taught me too. Jack Kerouac, whose huge manuscript in the bag was the "great American novel," smiling, helping me tap another sauce pan to Perez Prado, asking me about Chesterfields, glad to have me there listening to the records, to the big talk with brother John, gently tolerating my staying too long and finally easing my awkwardness in leaving—me trying to stand without them seeing, wanting to fade out behind their shouts about Lawrencian prophecies, "You have to leave, Liz? Come down again and we'll dig more mambo. Okay?" Bopper, genius, Beat king, enigmatically sweet fellow.

There were evenings of Jack too. I am sitting next to Edward Stringham at a party. My mother had asked John and Marian to look after me as she was going somewhere for the night. I sat now on the edge of the sofa. The fridge was across the way and I scrunched down on the edge, gauging the space to the door—a few steps through the entry hall—and out—if I got scared or embarrassed. With enough people around I could sneak out invisibly—an inconsequential breath of air inhaled by this stormy original gang of John's and then exhaled without notice. But I wanted to *be* there. I wanted to *see*. My eyes were wide. I could feel my eyebrows pulling them up, up in expectations of wonders.

In came a blond young man—straight hair falling over his forehead, full sexy lips pressed back in a smile, lean face, high cheek bones making slits of his eyes—an Oriental look when he started to laugh as everybody applauded his entrance. "Ah, Lucien, here at last—our own faded jonquil!" He got down on his haunches right near me huddled there on the sofa edge, "Yeah! I'm here to bring complete disgrace and so honor the lady of the house," or some outrageous thing. And he nodded, genuflecting with his cigarette to Marian, who laughed in his face. His voice was deep and raspy like the sound of loose stones being run over. He was exquisite. All these men were handsome in their ways—Edward, Alan H., Roger Lyndon, Jack, even Allen Ginsberg with his dark skinniness and thick, expressive lips. But this fellow was the diamond in the necklace. "Lucien Carr, of course," whispered Edward in my ear. Edward was courtly and never neglected me. He looked over at Lucien, amazed by his presence. It seemed that everybody in the room—twenty or so people—for the moment was in love with Lucien. It was the beauty—purely the beauty. How proud they were to call this beauty their own—all of them saved by this murderer-angel of light.

Then, of course, the party struck up again. I remember noise, immense amounts of booze on the table, the floor. In a corner by the French windows young men were passing skinny cigarettes to each other. All the girls were pretty with dark hair, in tight bodices and full skirts, all of them flirtatious and knowing and not nervous about the guys. There was a young man jerking his torso up and down in front of the phonograph—smoking, with bent head tunneled into the blare of Dizzy Gillespie, who skittered down from the stratosphere in frenzied glee. The young man was talking to Dizzy incessantly, noiselessly, his lips moving as fast as Dizzy's horn. Mayhem surrounded him, but he was sealed off by invisible electronic currents, Dizzy and the fellow with the bump on his nose, communing together: "That's Neal Cassady, Liz. He just arrived with his gang from Denver." Edward was again seeing me stare. Neal—long talked of by John as the wildest of them all. For a moment Diz materialized and stood high over Neal with his trumpet angled to heaven. John had said that Neal made things go, saw that the world turned in the "right sweet way" every minute. For a second Dizzy shimmered there above the phonograph. Neal was a magician—to be worshipped and feared.

Allen Ginsberg was standing near the windows. He wore huge round glasses—dark owl's eyes, a head that narrowed up to a mat of high black hair—in profile his head came down long in a straight line. His thick lips were sexually suggestive. He paid little attention to me when I'd seen him on other occasions. But when he did look at me, it was like he was seeing something strange inside me that I knew nothing about. Then he'd ignore me. Now he was by the window, and he had thrown his shirt away—maybe out the window, you didn't know with him—and let his pants drop and stood in his underpants. John was near and put his hand on Allen's arm and said something. Allen giggled in a way I'd seen before. There seemed to be great dramas going on inside his head that required his full attention. Now leaning his bony washboard chest far out the window— just as those maniacal fire engines reached their crescendo in front of the building—Allen screeched higher and louder and ended in a falling howl as they faded off.

Then everybody fell to with gusto. They collided and toppled in each other's arms to couches and to the floor. They acted out and shouted wild truths to each other: "Marian has just gone off to the bedroom with Tom, and John's forehead is knitted in angst and huge *guilt*! He is the only man on earth who feels guilt for his wife's transgressions. Hooray!" "My New Year's resolution is to love God for his absence—it is his very absence that is so endearing. We must love him for leaving us." "He hasn't left us—he is the long straight yellow line in the road—and we are all safe in his hands!" "You are God, of course, Neal, and we are safe, in time, hurtling down the highway of the world toward grace, in your hands!" "Oh, I cry for God, leaving us—look, look at the rue in his vanishing face, pining over his unrequited love for us. His heart is broken. It is so clear that we don't need him anymore." "Oh, shut up, Allen. Turning your feeling of rejection into his—he just doesn't love your nagging, obsessive soul." "See, he's an angel shining on Neal who moves us onto the road of ecstasy! See, like Al running up Lexington to score some weed—heading through joy!" "Or like Jack scowling at the bedroom door with jealousy—as John's best friend *he* should get the prize of his wife."

John had told me that this was the climax to every good party, but I didn't know how to think these paradoxical insights, much less shout them, and simply said to Edward who was still sitting next to me, "This is a great party! So amazing!" But Edward was staring at his lover, George Wickstrom, who was sharing benzedrine inhalers with the dark girl next to him. Then I snuck out the door—invisible at last—and went upstairs.

I was tired, but my heart raced and I didn't know what to do with myself in the empty midnight apartment. Too late to play my records since the tenant downstairs would complain. But I had to find my own "end of the night" that John talked about all the time. So I turned on Mom's radio that sat on the card table and it began picking up far away places until I happened on Radio Moscow. How wonderful! I loved Russia anyway—the promised land of equality and love—and hated what I saw as American bullying and warmongering. I was happy now to find my own little connection, my own silly truth.

Someone knocked at the door. I opened it to Jack. He came in with his half-smile and his look of the shyest, cutest boy in town. "What happened, Liz? You snuck off. What are you doing? Ah, the radio. What've you got on?"

"Radio Moscow."

"Hey, listen, Red Moscow! Let's dig here alone with Red Moscow in the middle of the night. Yes!"

We listened and didn't talk for ten minutes as the funny Russian voices throated in from far off. "The party get too wild for you? That's okay. So you came up alone." It was all okay, it seemed. I didn't have to tell him that there was something about everybody down there in 4C that thrilled and frightened me—Lucien's beauty, Neal's magic, Ginsberg's inner dramas bursting out, the girls' savvyness with the guys, even kind Edward's stare at George with the benzedrine. But now sitting alone with Jack, the lover of endless pretty women, I was not afraid.

For one thing, it seemed that my silly little Soviet truth was okay. Jack didn't scorn it. He truly must have safeguarded all creatures. He sat in a chair. I was on the couch. After a half hour he got up. "Better get back." I walked him to the door, grateful for his attendance to my funny girlish passions. But in the hall he did what I really wanted him to do. He took me in his arms and kissed me a good soft lover's kiss—long, full, with turned head and tender heart. The answer to every girl's prayer. He held me a while, deciding something, and then he bounded down the stairs and over the railing and looked up. "Not now, Liz, but I'll see you again. Now go to bed with Red Moscow." He blew a kiss and disappeared into the uproar.

I did see Jack again, a lot. He was there off and on for the next four years or so, and I learned much from him. Though I was never to get involved with him, I carried on a secret love affair with him in those years which became a background texture of my life, like all the little flowers and trees and fields behind the hunters, the virgin, and the unicorn of medieval tapestries. My dramas stood up front like those characters, taking up my time and my thoughts and feelings. And there in the back the little Jack-thing lay, filling out the picture, adding its suppressed lesson of loneliness, the background of my ongoing dramas, where I came to believe that he was the most important person I would ever know.

By the time of that evening when Jack and I listened to Russian radio together, I had gotten in the habit of knocking on John's door on empty afternoons when my high school of desire had finished for the day. John had always been very kind, and I can't recall him ever brushing me off or refusing entrance. I can't think why, since I didn't add much to the talk; perhaps it was his odd restrained love of me and the art of "digging" that widened my eyes and filled me with such damned silent eagerness, the "digging" that John and Jack had taught me, after all. I would always sit on the end of the couch close to the fridge and the hall. John would be here and there, manning the phonograph from a chair pulled out from his desk near the window. But it's not John that I now see on those visits. It's all Kerouac, all Jack, always on the chair or at the end of the couch. Always the same.

One afternoon (I can't remember the year) Jack was there with a black girl sitting up tight against him. He had his arm around her. He couldn't take his eyes off her and giggled softly in that sly, embarrassed, repressed way he had—but this time over this beautiful brown girl he had in his arm. She was brown and exotic and sat there, strong and quiet—a black queen, Jack's new queen. I remember her hair now as flowing and soft—funny, I thought, for a black girl. So what? Of course, she was everything I wasn't—confident, prettier, older—and black, damn it! I hated her, and I had never conceived in my leftie heart of hating a Negro! But she had Jack's arm around her and his thigh against hers and his tender, pained eyes all lit up and making love to her. Damn it, those Jack-things were mine! Oh, I had had all my crushes, and by then was probably beginning to sleep with one, though he was probably not one of the most fiercely desired, but in the background of all that there were the little flowers of Jack, belonging to *me* in perpetuity.

So I sat like a piece of granite, nodded at the queen and ignored Jack and looked angry and definitely didn't *dig*. I was lost inside my futile love-girl humors, and I wasn't nice to Jack and his new girlfriend. They didn't care and brushed it off as lone girl blues and went on their loving way. In the midst of their ongoing talk with John, himself just introduced to Jack's latest love, I slunk halfway up from the couch and said, "So long," and Jack asked with a wicked smile, "What's wrong, Liz?" smiling, knowing. I left. My own newly wicked heart was broken for the moment—and mad. The damn Negro girl—Billie Holiday in the flesh—had him—and how could anyone ever compete with Lady Day![8]

Another time—it seems to me it must have been after, but these are sense-points on my compass, so I can't vouch for their chronology since all I see in my recording eye is a chronology of feeling—another time when I went down to 4C, I saw Jack with a new girl under the same arm on the same couch. This time I was cool. I wasn't thrown into the raw cesspool of youthful rage and rejection. The girl was pretty—long black hair in a pageboy, the ends smoothly curled under; eyes of nervous little lights; thin, fleeting lips in the Italian/Irish mode—doors to a fragile heart that would crack if you pained her—and skin white, white and thin like lace. She was a fragile girl, and by contrast I felt tough and even a bit the better. Oh, she was older (weren't they all?), knew the mill all right, and I learned later that she was an unfortunate leftover slip of debris abandoned in Cannastra's apartment. "She knows the score of this town and these guys, but they'll break her," I told myself.

Jack introduced us. "Hi, Liz. This is Joan Haverty from Chelsea, and we're going to get married soon. Joan, Liz, John's gone little sister." And I felt strong. Jack was a nice simple guy, and simple girls like this Joan-person rolled over in a line for him, but he was a raw, simple genius writer, and fragile girls couldn't get their simple arms around all *that* for long. "Of course, I'll never get Jack," I sat there thinking in a new smug confidence. But my lonely nights of

---

8. Editor's Note: Some readers may assume that the woman that Elizabeth Holmes met was Alene Lee, the Native-American/African-American girlfriend of Kerouac's upon whom the character Mardou Fox in *The Subterraneans* is based. But she was not. Kerouac met Lee in the summer of 1953, after John Clellon Holmes had moved out of 681 Lexington Avenue.

whistling Charlie Parker's tripling runs up and down from heaven and "falling down to Robert's Auto Body and Fender Repair" with Symphony Sid, "the all night, all frantic one" that we listened to on the radio, gave me better credentials to at least "dig" Jack in all his simple profundities than this girl, so worried looking and taken by his beauty and his tender heart.[9]

Besides, by this time I had had my own experiences with Jack. I finished high school in January 1949, just two years of it, at age sixteen. So for the empty spring semester before college in the fall, and seeking always to avoid office work, I went to the New School for Social Research on Twelfth Street. I took three or four courses with huge, puffy names—one about philosophy; another in sociology, featuring the work of Herbert Spencer; another on literature of the modern consciousness—all profound and important and abstract, and all in a name. I took a semester of course titles and quickly began cutting classes—although I do remember sitting often in the top row of an amphitheater lecture hall and listening to a tiny, important, white-haired man way below wowing us to astonishment with philosophical tedium. I went down to the school four evenings a week, and, of course, I ran into Jack Kerouac. John and he were taking classes for the G.I. Bill money, and they were the prize class-cutters of the school—I never saw John there. He didn't seem to bother to show up at all. But Jack wandered around the lobby many nights like I did, digging the scene, rustling up later night action. We went for coffee a couple of times. He always smiled and sought me out with questions, but it was mild amusement for him and he was distracted.

One night I took him up to see my sister Lila. She was nine years older, striking, a blonde, and in and out of New York in those years with her second man, Don Vance, from Malibu, whom she had left her husband for. They wandered around, not settling easily—hitch-hiking, getting jobs on the run. He wanted to write, she could model and work as a receptionist in fancy beauty salons. Living the beat life really. But my sister was *not* beat. She took everything heavily and

9. Editor's Note: Jack Kerouac married Joan Haverty in November 1950 and the two separated in 1951.

didn't laugh much, and when she did, I thought she was angry at something, and I'd get nervous not knowing what it was and if it was me, center of the world as I was in those days. But she was beautiful with the kind of bone structure that crushed men. They idolized her. Not a cigarette passed to her lips without being lit—zip. Her guys never looked directly at anyone else in the room, only at her. I was amazed. It stumped me. They wouldn't even look at me. Don kind of flirted around the edges of John's gang when they were in town. But Lila always held back—was hard and severe about excess—booze, tea, bop, sleeping around. She was tame about music and liked soft stuff, like Nat King Cole and Garner's "Misty." Young as she was for such bitter feelings, she found many things "despicable" and used that word so often that I eventually came to be physically afraid of it and still never use it.

But that night, Jack knew she was in town. "Let's go see her, Liz." So we went to the studio on Twelfth Street where she and Don lived. It was a big room with a high ceiling and nice lights. Don was silly in his Hollywood way, but smart and literary and he liked jazz—cool West Coast music. He had full wavy hair parted in the middle, was tall and very thin, and had thick wet lips that grinned involuntarily, producing his Hollywood veneer. His long, thin fingers held long Pall Malls. Lila was statuesque, cool, tempting—and softer in front of the new handsome, talked-about Jack. Flirting a little in the heavy, serious way she had, she said, "We hear you've written a great novel. I must read it sometime . . ." and blah, blah, blah. I sat silenced as usual by the big sister with the hard verdicts.

When we left, Jack said, "You're mad, I can see it, Liz."

"Well, okay, but she gets them all. Her guys don't even *look* at anybody else. They're her slaves. Damn it!"

"Okay, Liz, you're being silly. She's a very pretty woman. Why shouldn't they slave around her? A pretty woman is the world's greatest prize. Come on."

How cruel he was because he knew how put down I felt. But then, "Relax, kid. You're not there yet. Late bloomer, funny, pouty, nice kid."

I had my own comeback:"Well, I'll tell you, she *hates* Billie Holiday!'"

He giggled and jogged along beside me to the subway."You're so funny. In your mute way, you do dig, though."

Another night, 1949, Jack says to me in a crowded lobby on Twelfth Street at the New School,"Hey, Liz, what's up? You going to that big philosophy class?" in his usual low, intimate tone.

"Do you want to go to a party? Some people are going to Ginsberg's later. It'll be interesting new kicks for you, a lot of funny people. Do you want to come?"

"Well, I don't know, I don't really care ... so ... I don't know ... I'd like to ..." I was furtive and scared, but eager as hell. Jack was asking me to a party—and not at John's!

"Then come on. John'll be there later. You'll be okay."

So we get on the IRT at Union Square. Not talking much, Jack smiling that sly, winsome, puckered smile, me with great pumping glad-girl heart in the subway with this gorgeous genius-writer sitting next to me, taking me to a party. We get off at Seventy-seventh Street, I think, and walk east to York Avenue. Dirty New York buildings line the street, dim and empty with gloomy lights here and there and fire escapes and dark doorways leading into rancid hallways and up stairs that always slant in their old-age dereliction.

Even as late as 2003, I've walked on New York avenues that still have the same look. Just walk along upper Madison Avenue—Manhattan's own Faubourg St. Honoré. Force your eyes above the Diors, Fauchons, Guccis, and there you will see the old true grimy face of New York that used to look out from all the avenues—except Park and Fifth—the rectangular windows unwashed for decades, the sills and frames peeling, the brownstones worn out under their soot, the upper three and four stories frowning down with all the grief of neglect. Ah, New York! Its deep, ugly heart still shows here and there. Today on the side streets you escape into the new fairyland of little trees and quiet buildings with beveled windows in the doors and scrubbed and painted brownstones—the air breathing soft and sedate—the neighborhoods encased in the peace of money. Ah, New York, you say, wears the richest face on earth.

But then get back on the avenues—Amsterdam above the coffee houses and glassed-in sidewalk restaurants (on every avenue now), and Second above the markets and kitchen stores, and Madison above the richest emporiums in town. "In New York," an old painter friend of mine used to say, "look above the eye-line. That's where New York bares its heart." That's where he would point out all the curlicues and cupolas, rows of Doric columns fronting an upper story, pediments over windows, baroque figures, gargoyles, a row of blue tiles, inlaid squares of mosaics. Yes, they're there. You look up ten or twenty floors, and there is grace in the air. But there's another heart of New York—a heavy dead heart that sits brooding over the arteries of commerce, both east and west. The arteries flow with money under the old left-behind heart of the city. You look up and face the dirty window, colorless curtains, a bare light shedding gloom from within, a flower pot on the sill that long ago gave up on the sun. People live here and there above Ralph Lauren, Louis Vuitton, maybe some pay handsomely for the privilege, others enter their fourth decade under rent control and have given up getting the plumbing fixed or the frames painted or the windows washed. New York's broken-up heart—money racing up and down the avenues, buying up tomorrow's fashions, fancy chocolates and pâtés, home decor under the ancient heart of pitiless neglect. New York has a miserable scabby illness of the soul behind its racing made-up face—an illness that's never terminal, as if all the money passing streetside only maintains the leprosy below.

In 1949, when Jack and I gloomed in all eagerness up York Avenue, the grimy tired brownstones with the same dust, same dirt, same drear-spreading light bulbs housed young hearts beating with unheard-of original thoughts and pumping crazy visionary poetry, music, and painting through the arteries of the city and out into the hinterlands of America—Alan Wood-Thomas paying $29 a month to paint on Eighty-ninth Street, John Holmes paying $50 to write novels on Lexington Avenue, Charlie Parker paying $25 to play sax on Avenue B. And here we were on York Avenue, crawling up the sunless stairs to where Allen Ginsberg paid $15 to have visions that still haunt America to this day. Ah, now you can't transfix the world at $2000 a month. You can only imagine that the tenants left behind in those wounded upper stories along the money veins are as exhausted and visionless as the buildings are. Okay, we will get to that party, although, as you'll see, it will be aborted for me.

Jack pushes open the scuffed-up door, and we go through the usual dismal entrance/kitchen into the living room, all foggy with low light. Ginsberg smiles up through the haze, sly lit-up eyes gleaming in the fog, not getting up from an armchair where he would sit the entire time—a Merlin of York Avenue on his throne. He is dimly resplendent and gracious in greeting, and I like him as I never have before. He'd always been so agitated, as if his nerves were pushing him into all your secret, painful corners. Now here in his own upper cave where he controls the magic, he seems to find me sweet and welcome. "Hello, Liz, sit down with Jack. Russell and I are just having a quiet talk about the possibility of turning hell into heaven and thus saving heaven from Urizen, Blake's monster god, and the archons. But of course, Russell will have none of it, still orthodox as he is, his true sainthood un-self-recognized . . ." or some such huge theological truth that fills me with amazement so that I stare at him. Allen isn't impatient, and he doesn't expect any clever word from me, so he returns to graciousness there in the fog. "Oh, I'm sorry, Liz, this is Russell Durgin, a theological student from Pennsylvania, an acolyte in the cause of God and the girl he loves—a true martyr. Russell, this is Liz, John Holmes's little sister, and Jack, of course."

Russell is a gloomy presence over by the wall—vaguely beautiful and grave, lost in his devotions, it seems. There is beer, which I am given, and some quiet talk. No sign that a big party is about to happen. People arrive and grass is passed. I am too scared and just turn away slightly to avoid the joint coming my way, praying that I am not hopelessly square. It is a quiet party so far. Allen modulates the talk so that I sense a low-key exchange of revelations about huge eternal questions—though it may have been nothing but gossip. But something tells me that at least some of these people are deep and will surface out of the foggy cave of York Avenue to make their original stamp on the world.

Jack leads me to a small back room—maybe the kitchen again, with its own grungy light, and the one person there—a slight, short man with brown hair combed back and thin eyes and mouth turned down, a weary-looking man, exhausted really, and disinterested in the party out there, in all the music and the talk. Cool warmth with Jack and acceptance without interest of me.

"This is Herbert Huncke, Liz. How goes, Herb?"

"Just doing some cooking, Jack. She won't mind if I do. It's morphine, of course, I'm fixing, and she can watch me take it. You're young and new and I won't offer you any, and Jack here sticks to booze and grass . . ."

He ties a cloth around his upper arm and the blue vein pops out at the inner elbow, and he sticks the long needle in with great slow art, bending his head to watch, and he slowly fills up with peace, and then chats with Jack about Times Square and where Jack's going off to next with Neal and how commerce is along the street, etc., etc. The phone rings and Jack is called and I sit in the kitchen with Huncke, who pays me no mind but doesn't mind me being there with him either. Jack comes back and says that it was John on the phone and he was coming right up to take me home.

"I think he's worried about you, Liz. But it's okay. I told him— you don't mind all this, do you?"

"No, no, it's all great!"

"Well, maybe a little scary . . . but . . . well, well, it's big brother John and you follow him. He looks after you, okay, Liz?"

Soon, so soon, John is coming through the door and sees me sitting there with Huncke where there has been no talk, no irony, and no evil from any side, and a little ignoring from the famous junkie and real gentleness from the genius-writer. John says that it is time to go home and half-whispers to Jack, "What'd you bring her here for? I'll be back with Marian."

We leave and are wordless on the way home, where I go to bed glad that I had gone with Jack to the party and had felt Allen's graciousness in the foggy room where he was a quiet wizard and had sat alone with Huncke sharing his peace and had gone home with my brother John.

Before I was to see Jack again, there was a long break as I began living my own precocious version of the Beat life. I had graduated from high school, and I had lost the old cherry, but I hadn't noticed its passing. I got balled up between two fellows—one black, stocky, friendly, and tender like a comrade who lay me down on my mother's cot in the living room and handled me with care and took it as an offering to me. The other—white, tall, a brush of receding hair at twenty-two, a laugher and kidder, who lay me down on my mother's cot and took anything left in there as a quick offering to himself. I had watched as both unrolled the rubbers down their cocks. They had both paused in the petting to carefully perform this rite—black Roy doing it for me, white Val for himself. Both were funny fellows. (Everybody in those days laughed a lot and had good times around the city with atom bombs in the sky and iron curtains across the world and angry leaders bent on doing us all in.) Both joked, Roy to be close and warm, Val to keep his distance.

My period was late and I threw my life over in a fit—it was finished; I was done with it at sixteen. The boys backed off. I was glad since I didn't want anything from them. They weren't my crushes. It was all a tryout that left me high and dry on the other side of curiosity. My mother was worried. My brother, whom she must have told, was mad. I didn't care. I thought he should know that I was in on the game now—smoking, drinking in the bars, and no cherry. He was worried and mad, but his anger never came out in a direct attack like "Damn, stupid little sister! What'd you go fucking around for?" No, it came out tight-lipped, a raging impatience to my mother, which I thought I overheard: "Well, she'll have to work it out, learn her lesson. Doesn't know enough not to fool around with two guys like that! Leave her to heaven (or hell)." But, damn it all, sex was the most important experience in life. It was deep and real—like D.H. Lawrence said—and all John's genius buddies acted out and knelt at the altar of it! Now it was my turn. But it had fizzled, had not been deep, and I had not sunk down into the dark blood. (Oh, how he and Jack had gone on and on about traveling to Mexico and down into the deep blood, like Don Ramon and Don Cipriano in *The Plumed Serpent*, to rise up original men in a remade world. I listened for hours one day to them shout about their coming pilgrimage to Mexico to imbibe fresh energy from the fellaheen earth. I never slept until I bamboozled my mother into buying a big expensive hard cover copy of *The Plumed Serpent* that I still have.) Now I had watched as the faces above me jerked and went blank in orgasm. I was nowhere near. So, as the gods would have it, I got my period and smiled smugly at Val and gladly at Roy, and we went our ways. I had lost my cherry and not my innocence and still didn't know the big score that could whirl me over the edge and change my life forever.

During that spring in 1949, I hung around frequently with a friend named Howie, one of the six teenage boys at Rhodes, where I still lingered to meet people. I couldn't join John's gang, after all, so screw it—I'd make my own. It was easy. Howie didn't know the score either and therefore couldn't be a crush à la Tom Grady or Paul Salomon, and in place of sex, we substituted music. In the summer, I met him up by Lewisohn Stadium between Amsterdam and Convent avenues where we would sit on the highest stones of the amphitheater and listen to Lauritz Melchior, and afterward Howie got his autograph on his program. I tolerated classical music, which had been my mother's rapturous pastime for years. Howie sat in the bleachers at Birdland the night it opened and listened to Charlie Parker while I jolted my head forward and back and *didn't* approach Bird at the bar for his autograph. Howie was perplexed by the alto screeing, but he loved music as would any tall, dusky-faced boy with dark-wavy-hair-in-place and soft lips, with a beautiful, stately melancholic Jewish mother who played the piano and seduced him to it too, and no discernible father. Yes, Howie loved music in the prostrate way of all us crazy idolaters.

So for a few months music was our sex. We rhapsodized at our various venues, holding hands and making liquid eyes at each other as the notes raised us up to heaven—for all the world like we came together. Sometimes I saw John and Jack milling around at Birdland. John was cool, but still glad to see me there, his A student making the grade. Jack was friendly enough—never the brush-off from his attentive heart. And I was proud to sit with my tall, dusky Jewish boy—my very own—and grab his hand.

I had a nice time with Howie, no love-push on either side, just two pure young music sensualists. Roy and Val, with their loveless sex on the cot, had not marred me in the least—the acts had left no trace at all. I had even made a vow not to repeat the thing until I was driven to it by some nameless force—love, libido, fate, drink, the most gorgeous male body in the world (Jack occurred to me, but I knew he was out of reach and I would be too trembly to truck with a genius even if he came on.). So I didn't repeat it for four years. Hah! If only John had known how fanatic a Dostoyevskian I could be!

One night Howie suggested that we go to his house in Washington Heights. "We can listen to my records. You don't know Mahler. I've got all his symphonies. It's the grandest music in the world!" With an "okay," we walked into large, quiet, carpeted rooms flowing back in endless space with deep, cushiony, floral sofas and matching armchairs, glass-doored bookshelves, flowing drapery covering entire walls of windows, and a baby grand piano resting in a sacred area—a shiny, onyx altar. Everything subdued, hiding its money in the culture that's bred in the blood of ages. There would only be low talk in these rooms— no raised voices and not much talk at all since everything would be said with music—gravity and deep thoughts with Beethoven, merriment with Mozart, ecstasy with Schumann. Who would need words when notes communicated for us with such clarity?

We sat on the couch and whispered a little. Howie told me his mother had gone out for a long evening at Carnegie Hall and a late dinner afterward at the Russian Tea Room with some musician friends from the orchestra. We kissed, the first in the year that we had been friends—open, tongues—and he went for the breasts, flat, but still eager in their timid hearts, and down the waist and then up the leg past the garter snap and along the inner thigh line that quivered. And he put my hand on him, strong and stretched in the bulky tweed pants he always wore. Soon we were touching soft and hard hot skin. (I hadn't touched Roy and Val—they hadn't needed it, damn them, denying me the most astounding, thrilling touch in the world—the hard, pulsing thing encased in hot cellophane skin wrap that moves with the grasping fingers up and down, helpless inside the sentient hand. Criminal sex-teachers they had been, after all.)

Howie wanted me to grab and hold on and move for dear life, just as I wanted him to keep doing what he was doing there between my legs. He was rubbing something I, in the innocence of all my second-hand knowledge, didn't know I had—some tiny point there that all of me—legs, arms, stomach, bottom—was rushing toward—all converging as we kissed ourselves unconscious, and the little point could hold it all and under his quickening finger push me—budding brain, unformed heart, untried flesh—push all of it up and out just as all of Howie broke out and dropped a white stream on my hand. For a tiny second the gangly Lizzie was gone—whew! That night I climbed to the top of the tree of knowledge. Now I knew what the older guys were talking about. You probably couldn't ever know more than that. Howie forgot to put on the Mahler symphony. In the dead hush, Howie, who had masturbated for a couple of years, and I, who had slept with two fellows—we both, without the benefit of intercourse, lost our innocence.

So late that summer when I came back from a month in Arizona and John took me down Lexington Avenue to a bar where he was meeting Jack, I went without a thought. I had drunk in a lot of bars—you could drink legally at sixteen in those days—and had learned to drive in Arizona and had come across the country alone on the train and had slept with two guys and was going to NYU in September and it would be fun to see handsome Jack again, who had also just come back from the West.

He and Neal were there in a booth with two dusky grinning cowgirls—tough-talking laughers, unhung-up—party bed pals, I could tell. "Hi, Liz, meet Dusty come all the way from Laramie, Wyoming, to meet us," said Jack, jovial and clearly having the greatest kicks with these two western knockouts. Damn, damn, damn! Yes, I knew a thing or two by now, but I couldn't laugh and have kicks and not give a damn like this Dusty and her pal who could wrap these guys around their weathery, fetching fingers. I could never catch up to Jack and John and that gang who were always up ahead teaching me and then shedding me like a useless coat at the change of season. I brooded in my beer. They didn't care and rollicked on together. Jack looked annoyed at me and then forgot it. I was mad. But finally I didn't care either and said later with Billie Holliday about "havin' that man," to hell with it!

Chapter 4

Neal Cassady

—— During these years when I was fourteen, fifteen, and sixteen, I had developed my whistle to a strong and fluid art. I could often go as high as Bird without lowering the octave, and my speed had been perfected on both Bird and Dizzy until I could keep up with the fastest solo I knew, Bud Powell's "Tea For Two," without the breaths knocking me off. I practiced my art for at least two hours every day. Even smoking almost a pack a day of Chesterfields, I had the stamina for the longest solos on twelve-inch discs and a sound to equal Dizzy's most gleeful shrieks. One afternoon, probably in 1949, I was alone and learning Wardell Gray's solo on "Blue Lou" that he had recorded with Erroll Garner in 1947. It was my then-current three-minute door to total afternoon solitary bliss. How quietly, lazily the music climbed up a notch with each version of the song. Three times he would consummate a delight by coming to the end—only to ride again, as though the last notes only cued him to a still prettier way to tell the tale. Oh, the slow natural lilt of Wardell carrying you along on a spring breeze, balancing on air like hawks above hills. I had played it for some time and was whistling most of it now without getting hung-up by Garner's bonking piano chords. He had thrown me off-track so often, causing me to switch off a looping Wardell phrase to throw in a too-loud step of Erroll's. Damn him with that clunky beat of hiccups. I had to steel myself to tune him out and pitch my tone to the lovely swerving currents of tenor sax. I was close now to mastering it.

I was sailing along nicely with Wardell and let the record play while I went to the door to let in Neal Cassady and Luanne and Al Hinkle who told me they were looking for John or for Jack at John's. Did I know where they were? He should be in soon. And usually was home about now, I thought, late afternoon, before Marian got home. "Well, yes, okay, how 'bout we wait here for a while? You've got some gone sounds going," Neal answered back. He had bushy faded red hair, a wide strong body, waist and arms in the light summer shirt that hung over his pants. And those sexy lips—shapely and spreading nicely in a smile of many white teeth under a bumpy nose. (Why do we lose lip flesh when we age? Old men with their lips gone, leaving a hard pencil line across their faces. When the lip flesh sags away, it's time to call it quits—nothing to lick and kiss and love with—just the angry line to spit out bitter bullets of sad life ironies.) So Neal smiled with bright, crafty eyes.

They followed me all the way back to my room where Wardell was still playing, about to give way to Garner. I put the needle back to the beginning and the three of them stood above me. Luanne seemed young, blonde, and a bit bored. Al was just tall and goofy, a good-humored American kid. Neal was the brains, the head of the gang, the leader whose roving curiosities had them tacking in the wind to keep up with him. I started whistling involuntarily and bouncing on the bed where I sat. Neal bent his head toward the phonograph, but studied me with sly side glances and a smile around the edges. I was obviously a funny, weird little untried cunt. Such lingo shone out of those canny blue eyes.

At the end of the solo, his attention abruptly turned away and ahead. "Okay, Liz, after that utterly gone tenor, we must move on ahead. Got to make some connections. Tell John we'll be at Allen's by 6:25 for thirty-five minutes. Okay, little girl, keep whistling with Wardell—the very most ultimate tenor! Thank you!" They left after approximately five minutes—a crisp use of time and not a second more.

I'd been hearing a lot about Neal—how he was this wild guy who blew in and out of town from Denver or San Francisco and was Jack's buddy and revered love-brother. For a while John talked about him all the time. This was obviously the season of Neal, as there had been the season of Bill Cannastra and the season of Gershon Legman. It was clear by now that Jack, in particular, and Allen Ginsberg were for all seasons. But the real mad men who broke all the rules and thought the most deadly or ecstatic thoughts took hold of John in binges. Now it was Neal darting through the room under the skylight like a 100-horsepower engine—one of those Buicks or Cadillacs he glommered on to—catapulting across the continent, eating up its towns and rivers, its deserts and mountains in two- and three-day feasts. He banged all the girls coast to coast and had a wife here and another one there and girls waiting in New York or Salt Lake or L.A. to be the next one.

Mom looked a bit reserved about this wild libertine that John conjured up in her living room during those evenings. She disapproved in silence, while I remained strangely exalted in silence at these tales. The wildest specters John brought upstairs to 5D always did this to me. His small eyes behind the horn rims were dots on the telegraph machine that picked up all these mother/sister silences, and he became more and more brazen and impatient to break our barriers and make us see the Beat apocalypse at hand—St. Paul of 681 exhorting us to blow open our minds to beatitude. These monologues were his epistles admonishing us to bow before the new order—to see the light.

I was scared, ready, and converted. But it took some rage to shake my mother. "What's the matter, Mom? Neal's not a dark, sinister criminal, robbing, killing, and raping women. He's a joyous, open hero of the west, adventuring and bringing *life*, rattling the bones of the dead until we all rise from our graves 'and aspire' to his holy grin. Oh, the girls get mad sometimes and jealous, but mostly they're eager to roll over for him. He loves them all and he loves jazz and tea and cars and *moving*. And he's totally focused on each act of life as it comes—getting the car, connecting for pads to stay in, for tea for the night, on getting gas and road food with his last two dollars.

Listen, we were in the car the other day heading up to Stringham's. He streaked into a corner gas station. He had Luanne go in and flirt talk to the guy with questions while he pumped the gas and even took time to wash the windshield and she came out, got in, and we streaked out without a whisper. Jack was huddled down behind the seat, but I was *amazed*. Awed by this act of clean, natural prowess. 'In furtherance of our evening joy-plans of obtaining the requisite grass by way of elegant Edward through his low-voiced, spaced-out George with his slynesses and zaninesses that will score us our ecstasies for this very next hour! Gas in the car and money for the tea and Stringham beautiful food joys and epiphanic Bartok gonenesses on the record player! Yes, yes, yes! Cutting through here on 113th, 7:50, and we're there!' And he's barreling across town, dodging cabs coming at us, going the wrong way on a one-way street. Don't you see! He knows life, he knows time, he always says, and he's completely unafraid!''

Mom was doubtful. But I was wide-eyed and not doubtful at all. Brother John was very persuasive when he had a message like this, as if he had seen a fabulous truth decked out in the flesh and it made him free. His voice would rise in declamation like the demagogue who wrenches you kicking and screaming into his vision. His gleams were magnified by the thick lenses, his irritations vanishing inside his talk as he lit one Chesterfield on the nub of another pressed there between tight tireless lips that paused only for the quick intake of the holy new cigarette.

There was a black table in the fireplace cut low by John himself with graceful curves (I have it to this day—still a coffee table, but, damn it, without the ashtray of prior friendly consort.) and the glass bowl there was abundant with his baby white nubs pressed into mats of blackened feverish ashes—the fallout from the bombs of his tales. It was wonderful, and I would go about dazed and knotted in brooding over the meanings of these epistles from my own sage in 4C—how Neal could figure in my backdoor little life and why he was instantly so important to it. Neal Cassady, who I had only seen twice up to that point, would haunt my building consciousness more than either of the two men I had slept with. Ah, the power of storytelling. John was an astute and mesmerizing practitioner of the art.

I did see Neal another time that summer. He came to dinner with
my mother, John and Marian, Lila (alone for some reason), and me.
Neal, wiry with the bony face and bumpy nose, and the dirty red hair
planted in waves on a head that came down straight from a high line
in the back (I didn't like that kind of male profile—it seemed hard and
flawed and marred my attraction to all men who had it. Oh, I loved
the lovely curve outward and then gracefully into the neck of dark-
haired gorgeous fellows like Jack.), loped along widely with us, swinging a suitcase—he was on his way out of town—a hand in his pants
pocket underneath the loose, gaily printed summer shirt. His head
was down, but I knew he was eyeing my sister Lila and directing soft,
pointed comments to her. He was paying no attention to any of the
rest of us, except John, who was necessary to his negotiations for the
coming night, to his mystical calculations for the maximum ecstasies
of the coming hours. Would he leave his bag at 4C, meet Luanne and
Al there, and crash there for the night? Would he park the car nearby
and connect with Jack and Allen for a final conference on further
occurrences? So John was *there* for him. But it was clear he had only
come on this family dinner, paid for by our mother at Joe's Restaurant
on Third Avenue, to put his mysterious, magical moves on Lila, the tall
blonde with the crushing bone structure and the tight ass. So he made
his moves, but it was all occult and deep-layered and seemed to give
him unseen rapturous kicks (or he wouldn't waste this prosaic hour,
would he?) even though he would not get in her pants. Of course,
with our several partings at 681, the game was over, but, by God, if
Lila didn't flutter a little and lose her cool—just for the split seconds of
"So long, have a good trip," giving him a secret involuntary smile, the
kind that escapes you at the peak of a flirtation. Neal, yes, the master
of all stages of seduction.

Well, to hell. He wasn't my type—that rusty hair, the straight-down
head, the handsome, canny eyes and sexy lips. What did I care? I never
saw him again. But I've read all the books and know all the legends
and even know some of the reason why he was the hero to three of
the most important writers of that mini New York apocalypse.

Chapter 5

NYU

—— I entered NYU's Washington Square College[10] in the fall of 1949 at sixteen and, for all my jazz and literature knowledge, quite dumb. All this learning from older "brothers" and resident geniuses and brilliant wits set me sailing into college careless of the winds. I had this big John-wind, after all, hard at my tail to carry me through, and it all seemed either easy (comp essays I tossed off—I had studied three years of Spanish—no need to take *it* seriously) or stupid (drab biology lectures and smelly labs and foul Bunsen Burners). Second-string, hashed-over stuff with no adventure or discovery about it. I languished through the days, drinking a lot of Cokes in the coffee shop on Waverley and smoking with my young freshmen compatriots, all from "ordinary kid" high schools. I was bored and missed my high school with its fast classes and smart older guys and told my mother that college was a snap, never as hard as old Rhodes had been.

Oh, I mourned Mr. Perry's mustache, bald head and nearsighted eyes, and leather elbow patches on tweed jacket and his quizzical communion with the ceiling and his sweet air of being long pickled in literature. So I decided to perk up my comp class, taught by a studious,

---

10. Editor's Note: Washington Square College was established as part of NYU in 1914, housing the arts and sciences divisions. It was merged with University College in 1973.

dusty, lumbering, dry PhD student cautioning us about organization and development and ignoring world-shattering perceptions and epiphanies of the spirit. I leapt to the page and wrote emotional narratives about going to the Three Deuces on Fifty-second Street and watching Charlie Parker at Birdland, all loaded with strident declarations and absolute truths. Then I'd knock his dried-up argyle socks off with my meetings with Jack Kerouac, the unacknowledged greatest novelist in America. Jack was personal history now and I would use him for all he was worth.

Not much, as it turned out. I got Cs and C-s on all those fervid opuses. The tedious grad student—earnest and mumbling and trying to support a wife and baby on his teaching assistant salary—pointed out all the deficiencies: nothing but wild opinions and emotional outcries, no details to back them up, fancy flights of pretty words, hyped-up stories—"Certainly not expository essays, Miss Holmes." So I sat down and wrote some boring discussions about the differences between high school and college, the step-by-step process of deciding a major, the advantages and disadvantages of work versus college, my purpose in life, and blah, blah, blah. Feeling put down and bored by the whole effort, I pulled the grade up to B-. I flunked Spanish (I knew it all already and cut the class for weeks at a time.), and I memorized just enough in the lectures and cut up just enough frog to pull a D in biology.

But I got an A in world history because all we had to do was take notes on all the dates of wars and treaties and rulers and I really loved the saga of the world rolling on from destiny to destiny like a big bass drum booming along over the earth until it arrived right here and now in New York City. Sitting there above Washington Square, I felt part of the great march of events—New York in the fifties was the catbird seat of history. Besides, all we did in history class was listen to the expert give us the world, and we never had to say a word—for a whole semester we could sit mute. Of course, I had honed the art of listening and was by now a master of the clear direct look toward the speaker with never a flicker of distraction—no eye drifting off, no studying of fingernail, no hand-covered yawn, no empty stare.

I had the habit of full attention—the receptive eyes, the smile that recognized irony, the nod of the head at the exact point agreement was called for, the listening strategy that crawls smoothly inside the speaker's head and gears your responses to the dynamics of his tale (except if it was biology). Oh, yes, I knew how to listen.

I had also mastered in the small lecture hall of 5D the secondary art, complementary to it, of not talking. The teacher talked on and on, I looked steadily at him, laughing and nodding in sync with his narrative, and by the time he said, "Any questions?," we were closing the books and the bell would ring and he looked vaguely in my direction for the confirmatory half-smile I always had ready. With a memory that photographed the facts from my notes and an ease with strutting out the three effects of the Treaty of Ghent and the four reasons for the defeat of the Spanish Armada, I aced the tests and wrote a flawless term paper on the revolutions of 1848 and smiled at every sound of the closing bell and got my one A.

Of course, I loved literature and was repelled by English composition and finally read the great novel now out of the bag and in the stores, Jack's *The Town and the City*, and wanted to write tone poems to the falling leaves of autumn, the loss of home and innocence à la Wolfe and Kerouac. The lumbering grad student teacher was keen enough to see that I didn't know what I was talking about and that I was obviously ensnared by this handsome young would-be writer who was probably a drunk and up to no good with me.

As it turns out, everybody was wrong at some point in this freshman comp experience. First, my essays were crap, but there was an earnest seed of word and thought buried in it all. I had hated every small town I had ever lived in and was glad when my mother and father broke up and was jubilant when we left snotty Chappaqua with its neat divisions between the handsome perfect kids from Lawrence Farms and the scruffy ones from marginal areas—Italian town where Marian came from and off-beat back roads dotted with outlanders like us who rented. I was more jubilant when we took up housekeeping in 5D with the roaches and the tall vets at the school behind the Museum of Modern Art and my big brother John downstairs with the bebop and the crazy poets and writers and drunken pot parties. It seemed that the breakup of family and loss of home and community had all been gains for me. All that sad-lost-autumn business, all the Wolfe-Kerouac grieving, must have been buried too deep for me to get a handle on. I was clearly expanding my consciousness in ever-widening circles from the 681 center and having a jolly good time all the way. So those essays were threaded together out of whole cloth.

However, Mr. Grad Student was wrong too inside his basic insight about Miss Holmes. Jack was not yet a confirmed drunk and was a writer and was up to *only* good with me. And although I wouldn't know how to tell it for many years, the nuts and bolts of a good story were fitting together every day of my life at 681. But then, in the comp classroom in the Main Building of Washington Square College at NYU, they added up to a solid C. In spite of all that, I stuck to my pursuit of literature (to hell with comp) and declared an English major and then, to cover my losses, I made history a second major. After all, I loved those one-sided friendly conversations with history teachers, and I loved the world. How could I not, living as I did at the exact navel of the island that was the capital on which the world pivoted?

During my second year at NYU, I began to get a grip on the scene. The sophomore literature survey was closer to home. I also enjoyed philosophy class where some of the names John tossed around got filled out (Kant, Kierkegaard, Spinoza, Schopenhauer, Nietzsche). The teacher was a runty little man, young, with wispy hair and a way of hissing words through thick moist lips with what must have been a Viennese accent. His head was cemented to his shoulders—rigid—unable to move independently, but he was very earnest about his subject and half-smiled through his talk out of some secret sensual relationship to it. We thought him a bit ridiculous and were titillated by the faint aura of wickedness that hung about him.

He was a bachelor and lonely and a bunch of us began a teasing companionship—we'd go out for some beers and then agree to go to his apartment somewhere in the East Thirties. A clammy cramped little place where we drank some more and he played Beethoven and Hindemith for us. We were getting high and laughing, but he was still trying to teach: "You must understand the German soul and the angst that gives rise to its music, its philosophy, its evil." Then he made each of us, a mix of boys and girls, sit in his orgone box. He explained its workings, but I already knew what it was, having listened to John talk about the psychiatrist Wilhelm Reich and his theories of sexual energy. Each of us took our stint for a few minutes, and I for one know that I giggled. The girls came out grinning. He leered angrily at us. Clearly he had hoped that one of us might have gotten the vibrations and stayed the night with him. But he also wanted to teach us the value of this therapy. But there we were, a couple of silly teases putting down the professor—a lonely devoted monk of philosophy brought to nastiness. "Now, students, get out!" he yelled, and we scampered away.

By this time, I was beginning to come into my own and had begun to have new autonomous friendships—a girlfriend, Naomi Weinstein, who loved literature and was often smarter about it than I was and a good lit class with a group who met after class in the cafeteria and talked *Beowulf* and Sheridan. How much fun this congenial group had with *All For Love* by John Dryden, for instance. It was new and comforting to learn Brit lit in a community like this. Now and in a year more John and Jack would be current literary history, and how I, with my very own literary gang, traded on those names! Especially with Naomi, my literary buddy who smoked incessantly and cut the air with her fiery gestures and affirmed every statement with the word, "Definitely!" She was also experimenting intellectually with lesbianism and wanted to go to the famous dike bars on MacDougal Street and talked about making one of the prettier girls in the cafeteria. Naomi read *The Town and the City* after it came out, so I badgered her about my pal, Jack, and my brother, John, who was now writing a novel about his Beat friends. Naomi *was* impressed, though she was critical of all the Wolfean outbursts in the book. She was a good sharp Jewish girl not given to my craven fake romanticism. But Jack's lyrical face on the jacket was awfully seductive. Around that time, he was in the hospital with phlebitis, and Naomi and I trekked up north to Richmond Hill to visit him. At eighteen, we both had grown-up designs on the handsome writer. We stood outside the building, thinking of him in there, feeling our sexual hormones rising, and eventually deciding we couldn't really visit him in the right spirit. We never went in.

Jack had become history, a name to solidify my status as an initiate in the inner sanctum of literature. Later John would be as well. His first novel about the hired killer had been turned down, and both men wrote about the simultaneous rejection of John's manuscript and the acceptance of Jack's. I recall only that John had seemed to struggle and had probably lost interest in the Frankel book. Jack, Allen Ginsberg, Neal's crowd, Huncke, and the Times Square denizens had embroiled him in more burning dramas. The Dostoyevskean hired killer, a product of Yeatsean "midnight oil," must have faded into an abstract corner of his mind, which in turn was blasted away by the wild visionaries who stalked through his living room night after night. What a deadbeat Frankel must have become, a thoroughgoing reject, perhaps first rejected by John's own incipient talent. In any case, John was hurt and silent that afternoon, staring doomsday in the face over his cigarette when he told us about the final rejection. But he was soon again telling tales of Ginsberg's latest hallucinations, Neal's stash of tea in 4C with other outlaw paraphernalia, and Cannastra's final descent into hell. His monologues regained their fervor, his eyes once again lit up with his epistolic mission.

In college, I was now using all this material for my own ends. John's stories and my own experiences as a student of "Beat education" were taking on historical significance. A new generation had emerged, and the names I threw out in cafeteria seminars would have to be reckoned with. Jack Kerouac with his romantic opus and his cross-country buddy; Neal Cassady, whom he followed in a new Beat mission of America. Jack, who had married this Joan-girl whom I had seen nervous and on unsure ground in his arm in 4C. And out of the debris of Cannastra's Chelsea had risen the phoenix of Jack's first genius—the original unparagraphed typewriter roll of *On the Road*. John told me about it, and then I told others about it in the corridors of NYU. I retailed these wholesale goods for the price of a little collegiate status.

But I believed in my soul in the goods I was selling, though many scorned and found me endearingly obnoxious. "Here we go again— Kerouac and that damn brother who's always going to write a great novel and hangs around with a bunch of drunks and tea heads who yell 'Go!' at incoherent saxophones and squealing trumpets and steal cars and yell about everything being holy, while the world is blowing up because of capitalist greed and provocation, and goddamn, Liz, we've heard enough already!" This from my large and special Communist friend, Manny, a huge aging vet with tight black hair and a pock-marked face, who lumbered and laughed over my silliness about my brother and who regaled us with endless stories of self-denigrations and divagations—his cramped family home in the Bronx, his verbal portraits of pathetic mother and ridiculous father, stupid sisters, and idiot himself—all dribbled out in a high hoarse voice ripped through with his own hilarity. He had us all on the floor morning after morning with these strings of self-putdowns that could extend themselves until the bell called us to class. My Communist pal, thirty-three years old, a scarred comic giant who was in love with me, even though he thought I was an idiot. But he also saw that I was a serious idiot. Of course, I wasn't in love with him but with his vet pal Lenny, a taciturn cynical fellow who played Manny's straight man and was private and remote enough to be the focus of all my desire. So Manny knew I was an idiot, the way I prated about John and Jack and the way I quietly swooned around Lenny. After a year of my nonsense, he said to me over coffee somewhere, "You're a mixed-up mess, Liz. But you're okay. You have good values deep down." I was glad, even though at the time I had no idea what he was talking about.

Well, I did proselytize in those NYU days. I wanted people to know about the serious truths I'd learned from John and Jack about the extremes of experience, the discoveries (now with all the barriers blown away) that were giving us unheard-of freedoms—the freedom to bring jazz out of its old restraints and wrench old tunes out of their melodic patterns to create endless amazing variations, the freedom to write like Jack, who was writing the way Charlie Parker played his alto, the freedom to live wholly original, spontaneous lives that would yield astounding insights or nutty truths like Neal's saying "We know time—Everything's always all right." My friends thought I was goofy or, at best, an enthusiast, and a few put up with me for their own reasons—Naomi for literature, Manny for love. He thought I was a backslider from my early Bolshevism, the vestiges of which still clung to me, and tried to steer me back from my new alliance with what he termed the "intellectual, decadent lumpen." But I had already veered hopelessly away from the political toward the literary approach to life.

Chapter 6

Marian and John

——— My government teacher was a folksy blond young man from somewhere in the South, very liberal and eager to be in New York and excited to live in his small room in one of the faculty row houses along Waverley Place, where he would take a few of us to talk. An open genial fellow, he had a wide grin on his face for everything. He appeared to enjoy my exuberances, so one night I dragged him and a few others up to the big, beatest bar of them all—Glennon's on Third Avenue and Fifty-fourth Street.

I had been there before. John, in fact, had introduced me to it by declaiming, "We don't go to P.J. Clarke's across the street anymore—too self-consciously writerly. Since they filmed *Lost Weekend*[11] there it takes itself too seriously as the Third Avenue raw bar where the important writers hang out. Norman Mailer et al.—but even he slips across the street to Glennon's where the real filth is, where the real avant-garde Beat writers and weirdies go." They finally took me there, although Marian was doubtful, "Do you really think Liz ought to see that trashy dive? Everybody drunk and puking on the

———

11. Editor's Note: Based on the novel *The Lost Weekend* by Charles Jackson, the film of the same name was directed by Billy Wilder and released in 1945 starring Ray Milland and Jane Wyman. The plot of the novel focused on an alcoholic writer tormented by a homosexual incident in college; in the film, the writer's alcoholism is attributed to writer's block.

floor, whores at the bar, and old bums sitting pickled in the back booth? God, I can't stand it myself more than once in two weeks."

Marian was protective of me during this period, probably using my innocence as a cover for her own distaste for much of the wild life of dope, criminals, unruly roustabouts, and unsavory visionaries. Ginsberg never reached her with his mystical probing into everyone's dark corners and his nude Blakean antics—nor did Neal bursting in with contraband to stash in her domicile. "He's just a con man, Johnny, and you make him out to be some kind of prophet of the new life. He cozies up to every girl in town, bangs them, marries, and moves on to the next. Goddamn prick! Well, he's never put the moves on *me!*"

Marian was a tough little bird with a beautiful brown face and hair, a thin mouth that broke into a sideways smile against her will—brown hurt eyes that were defenseless even when she was angry. And she was angry a lot during these years—working two-bit jobs that barely kept them in beer and cigarettes and a few private dinners at the Ritz Food Shop up on Lexington in the sixties. The rest of the time she had to get by on the largesse of our mother who staked us to the family dining room—Joe's Italian Restaurant—and whose help was needed to pay the rent most months. She was demeaned in her home and family heart. At 681, on her forty-dollar-a-week secretarial job, she found herself coming home to loud bebop and a husband and assorted marginal guys banging on her pots, drunk on beer, glasses littering her rented kitchen table and her big glass ashtrays running over with butts and her rented couch draped with a dirty sheet where Jack had passed out the morning before, just before she had to get up with her own cigarette and coffee cup and grab her shoulder bag and swing her wide hips in the plaid skirt out the door—banging it in one defiant noise to her passed-out men, "Goddamn crash pad for every drunk in New York! My home!" She was mad, and she fought with her "Johnny" about it, quarreled and pouted and tried to hold the little line of home against the tide of chaos that was sweeping over their lives in the late forties.

But she was also a naturally brainy girl who perceived much of what was going on with these "nuts"—in a small believing corner of her heart, she must have thought they were on to something, disruptive and unsavory as they were. Like so many of us, she was soft on Jack—sweet he was in his soul, just as she was retro about the old family, hers Italian and his "Cannuck," as he called it—both nostalgic and simple of spirit. Outrageous as he was, she couldn't turn him out. Rumor had it that they had had an affair, and it's always made sense to me.

But more to the point, she believed in Johnny, that he would come through with some book that would see the light of publication. And, with her patience and good-humor fraying and unraveling periodically in these frenetic forties of weary work and disordered home, she lay up her store of belief for that happy day. She mused with Mom and me, often visiting us alone for coffee and smokes. Perhaps she found a bit of peace in 5D. My mother, or "Betty" as Marian called her, was always calm, reserved, and sympathetic with her; I was more talkative with her than with her awesome husband, my brother, chatting teenage girl stuff with her and longing for some hugs and kisses. She was a small affectionate girl in her brown Mediterranean soul, and I knew she wouldn't reject my arms around her when she left, businesslike as she could be, having to keep that crazy 4C afloat. I loved Marian. To this day, wherever she may be, she is my memory of the heart-sister of my adolescence. I wish her the kisses of many grandchildren in her old age, the other strong urge of her nature that eventually led her right.

So she protested my going to Glennon's, and she was right. The pride of utter filth and degradation there greeted you at the door with a knockout blow. I had been in bars—quite a few—with my own buddies. But this place put me on alert. There was no bottom line of decorum at Glennon's. You could shout as loud as you wanted. Guys could fistfight, could molest women, could piss their pants and break the john door, which was already broken anyway, and could throw their beers across the tables at the scarred poster of the Dublin Horse Show of 1937 on the back wall. The bartender was blandly indifferent, which many interpreted as encouragement. There was a jukebox, but live voices usually drowned it out. The booths were collectors of trash—torn papers with poems and phone numbers on them, the tables greasy with stale beer that seemed to accumulate from week to week. The night that I first went there with Marian and John, Montgomery Clift was at the bar—the beautiful star who was so decorous at the Dover Deli—shouting to the air in the back of the place and swinging his beer glass toward his invisible listener. I hunched in the booth, ogling and quietly terrified and feeling that, yes, this must be the public catbird seat of all the revolutionary action that John talked about. This was the anteroom to the night. This was where they all came to receive the public imprimatur for spiritual insurgency in order to sow the seeds for later night private exposures and revelations. Of course, sometimes they never got out of there and ended up on the tables or on the floor in their own pools of beer.

My consciousness was soon in overdrive. Marian saw and grabbed my hand. "Come on, Liz, let's get out of this hellhole. Johnny, try to come home before four in the morning and don't bring any hangers-on tonight. I mean it. I'm bushed from the week." Jack Kerouac, who was there as well, chimed in, "Even me, Marian, Cannuck and wop together?" He was drunk and winsome, but Marian stood her ground, "No, not even you, old frog bastard!" Then the sideways smile broke out, "Damn it," she said, flouncing up, bending, and kissing him on the cheek.

So that had been my introduction to Glennon's. By 1950, when I was a sophomore in college, it had all become history. I led the government professor and a few classmates up to Glennon's, having prepared them with my own elaborate exegesis, stressing the contemporary significance of the place, the meeting ground of the cutting edge avant-garde of our time, oh, so much more genuine and far-out than the Village hangouts, San Remo's and the like. But it turned out to be a boring evening. None of the first string of the cutting edge showed up, and we tried to be boisterous and vulgar ourselves as the place expected its clients to be. We did get drunk, and there were beers littering the table. We tried to break out of academic gossip, and the young professor was impressed enough to stagger and shout a bit. But let's face it—we were a poor imitation of the real thing. The old real thing seemed to have vanished across the continent.

For instance, John had written a book that would make those years—1948 and 1949—official history. After the rejection of the Frankel book, Jack wrote to him from Denver, Colorado, urging John to chronicle all the New York craziness of that time—all the parties, all the visions, all the music, all the astounding apparitions of Neal and his gang and Huncke, all that he had lived through, so much of which had taken place in his very own apartment at 681.[12] I only learned about Jack's inspiring letter in recent years. John had never mentioned it to either Mom or me. The only thing he said to us once, a few months after the rejection, was, "Marian said, 'Okay, John, why don't you write about what you know firsthand—all the discoveries, all the hysterics and crap you've just lived through—Jack, Neal, Allen, all of it. It could make a startling story. It's obviously excited you so.'" He was low-keyed, but I could see the expectant light in his eyes—a surprised flush of knowing he could do it, that it was there lying in his hand. Marian was there too and stood up to signal their departure: "Yes, I said to him, 'You know it firsthand, not some thirdhand, booky idea.' Anyway, Johnny, I know you can do it."

They left, and he did do it, and the rest is literary history.

I don't know how long it took John to write Go. Time is perhaps wrongly compressed for me here. The months went by. I plodded on from my sophomore to junior year at NYU. John didn't come up to 5D as much. Maybe I had already veered away from the heady days with him and all the happenings in 4C. Perhaps John was deep into the chronicle of it all. Perhaps the writing was flowing where the talk had flowed before. And Jack was gone on perpetual swings between San Francisco and Mexico City with only fleeting stops

---

12. Editor's Note: In a letter dated June 24, 1949, Kerouac wrote the following to Holmes: "I've been thinking about you and have come to a pass where I feel qualified to suggest that, among other things, you should write immense novels about everybody, using the New York scene and the New York types (this is, us). But on a more social plane. . . . I should like to see you invent a potpourri out of [Alan] Ansen, [Bill] Cannastra, Allen G. the people who come to your parties, the San Remo the bars, the mad parties, big swirling vortexes like [Dostoyevsky's] *The Possessed*, not concentrating too much on one individual, but painting a large impassioned portrait like Dickens, only about the crazy generation. (*Jack Kerouac: Selected Letters 1940-1956*. New York: Viking, 1995, 199-200).

in New York. My days were taken up with classes and long talky
rambles with pals to a Waverley bar and Italian joints on MacDougal
Street. I was becoming collegiate, intellectual, and a partygoer myself. I spent a year studying every Shakespeare play, including *Titus
Andronicus* and at least one part of *Henry VI*. I spent the same year
exhausting every facet of the Renaissance and writing papers on
most of the main thinkers of that time (John did write my paper on
Erasmus, which got an A and for which I am still grateful to him.).

I also delved deeply into Americana—definitely its history,
but mainly its literature. John again. He had said, for so many
years that to me it seemed literary law, that "Americans are the
great stylists of the novel in English. It is us that the French and
other Europeans read, not the dull British. They read Melville,
Poe, Twain, Faulkner, Fitzgerald. We are the ones with a tradition
of style, and we run the whole stylistic spectrum—the rolling,
elaborate Biblical rhetoric from Melville to Faulkner, Wolfe and
Kerouac and the spare bones of statement from Twain to Crane
to Hemingway. Read Americans!" Clearly, I was headed to every
course in classic American literature the school offered—Haw-
thorne and Poe, Melville and Whitman, Emerson and Thoreau,
Twain and Howells, and then all the moderns. In those days we
snooted Henry James as "just a fussy American Brit is all." We
were exalting America à la Jack—its freedom, its space, its originality. After all, we were chasing the barbaric yawp. With John and
Jack thrusting me through the starting gate, it was no wonder I
specialized in American studies, a field that was just beginning
to emerge. It surely accounts for my boredom with the required
English novel course (all the Richardsons, Sternes, Fieldings, and
Thackerays) I suffered through and often skipped and copied off
Naomi's exams and in which I barely managed to get a B by writing a decent paper on *Sons and Lovers* by the only Brit I liked. And
I actually loved him. After all, Lawrence was John and Jack's old
sex prophet of the new blood, and didn't he love American writers and disdain the "frowsty" old Brits? One of our literary bibles
was his *Studies in Classic American Literature*.

Elizabeth Holmes (Von Vogt), age 11, and John Clellon Holmes, age 18. Spring 1943. Chappaqua, New York. Taken by their mother, Betty Holmes.

Holmes, age 18, 1943, at the family's rented cottage in Chappaqua, New York. Von Vogt speculates that this stance was intentionally posed and was photographed by their mother.

Above: Photographs of Elizabeth Holmes (Von Vogt) on the rooftop of 681 Lexington Avenue. 1949. Taken in the same series as the image on the cover of this memoir.

Below: Pictures for graduate school applications. Spring 1954. Saybrook, Connecticut. Her mother's house and car are visible in the image on the left. In the image on the right, one can see John Clellon Holmes' house that was located behind his mother's, referred to on pages 77 and 116.

Betty Holmes, Von Vogt's mother. In her mid-forties. 1947.

John Clellon Holmes, ca. 1949–1951, the period chronicled in *Go*. Long Island.

John's first wife Marian, ca. 1940s. Von Vogt believes that this photograph may have been taken by Holmes in Chappaqua, New York, at the Holmes' family cottage during World War II while the two were dating.

John Clellon Holmes with Von Vogt and her husband Carl at their house in Nobleboro, Maine. 1982.

John Clellon Holmes and his second wife, Shirley Allen Holmes, on the patio of Von Vogt's Nobleboro, Maine home, ca. 1982. The two visited Von Vogt every year until Holmes became ill in the late 1980s.

The old 681 building—front door, open bare bulb.

Von Vogt and husband Carl with their sons, Steve (left), Paul (right), and son Mark behind the camera, in front of 681 Lexington Avenue, 1966. Stopping in New York City on their way to visit Von Vogt's mother in Saybrook, Connecticut, before heading north to spend the summer in Maine. The family lived in Chicago at this time.

Lexington Avenue as it looked in 1940. The skyline is markedly lower than it is today.

All three images: Sperr, Percy Louis. "Manhattan: 56th Street—Lexington Avenue." Photographic Views of New York City, 1870s–1970s. June 17, 1940. Photographs: Milstein Division of United States History, Local History & Geneaology, The New York Public Library, Astor, Lenox and Tilden Foundations.

681 Lexington Avenue as it appears today. The apartment building where Elizabeth Holmes (Von Vogt) and John Clellon Holmes lived is now a commercial building housing a shoe store and eyeglass shop.

Von Vogt's son Mark stands in front of the building in 2006, bottom right. Photograph courtesy of Elizabeth Von Vogt.

Top and bottom left images: "Views of 681 Lexington Avenue." October 2007. Photographer: Tom L. Milligan

The painting on the left is referred to in Von Vogt's memoir on page 142. John Clellon Holmes painted this image when he and second wife, Shirley Allen Holmes, moved to Saybrook, Connecticut, in the late 1950s. It was passed on to his mother and then, upon her death, to Von Vogt, who had always been impressed with the painting.

The ceramic plate on the right is referred to on page 142. Von Vogt kept the plate, which she believes may be of Catalan origin, as a memento of her brother's Saybrook home, where it had been displayed on the wall. October 2007. Photographer: Tom L. Milligan

Elizabeth Von Vogt today.
She lives with her husband
Carl and her one cat, Oxford.

Noblesboro, Maine.
October 2007.
Photographer: Tom L. Milligan.

Sometime in 1951 John came upstairs and gave me the manuscript of *Go* (then called "The Beat generation"). "Here's the book, Liz," he said with a spare humility, placing himself in his little sister's hands. "You know a lot of all this, so here it is." And he left.

I tore into it the moment he left and finished it in two days. With each page I was breathless and amazed. Here they all were—Jack, Ginsberg, Huncke, Neal, Luanne, Stringham, Cannastra—all the people I'd seen, all the parties I'd heard about as a high schooler in John's fervid and exhaustive monologues until they became mighty legends in the telling—Cannastra's demonics, Ginsberg's visions, Neal's mad dashes across the continent that he had made into his neighborhood. And here was John—no longer a mythmaker—now a confused and earnest young man writing abstract love letters to a girl from Columbia, Mira Kent, his intellectual comrade who he had talked to us about long ago. Here finally were John and Marian battling through their marriage—quarreling and jealous, always pulling at each other, so grave and serious and working at it. It was astounding to watch monologue, lecture, and declaration become fiction—Alchemy—the turning of the base metal of talk into the gold of literature. To me, *Go* was literature in the same class as the Wolfe and Hemingway I had read. I found it beautiful and oddly modest and terribly sad. The long agitated verbal afternoons would never have led me to expect this—these humble, hoping pages that brought together a whole world of unique people trying to forge new and strange ways of living in this dark and rainy city. Here John had come off his pedestal as lawgiver and moved now into my consciousness as a bona fide novelist. Being marked as I was—first by Mr. Perry at Rhodes School and then by John and Jack Kerouac, and after the fact, by my college professors—marked to be an acolyte of literature, I finished the book, sniffled a bit as I did at the end of my favorite novels, and thought John a genuine hero at last.

I was scared to talk to him. What kind of expert critique could I cough up when the book had lifted me beyond analysis or even fine insight? I thought it was great. I loved it. What could I say? There was no distance here, no detachment. I was in awe again before this new brother who was entering the ranks of literature. So I brought it down to him one afternoon and found him tentative and expectant. I shivered in my boots having rehearsed nothing to say. "It's great, John. I just loved it so much. I don't know—all the people in it—they all just seem so innocent." That was it. I spread my hands and shrugged my shoulders and, yes, became dumb as a stone. He was pleased, smiled, and didn't seem to care that I had nothing more to give. After all, this was the old Liz he knew who never went beyond monosyllabic approval—who just dug. "I'm glad. Thanks, Liz. I value your opinion. It's strange that you call them innocent—even the criminals. Interesting." I had to explore this on the spot, and I was never a good thought-and-word improviser. "I don't know. It's just that they all try so hard. They try to work everything out. It made me love them." That was okay. We fumbled a bit after this critique, awkward with daily exchanges, and I left.

I wondered too why I came up with the word "innocent" about all these people who had affairs and were unfaithful to partners, who stole cars and took drugs and robbed and quarreled and fought and saw God in a Harlem hall and ran around naked. I thought of the murderers in Dostoyevsky, the careless decadents in *The Great Gatsby*, the cruel old Ahab, the selfish Paul Morel in love with his mother and hurting girls. And, yes, something in the alchemy of literature turned their various guilts into innocence. But I didn't see it until this flesh and blood brother of mine took himself and his gang and wrote about all they did—every wart and hurt and crime—and washed them clean in the telling.

Of course, I was a pushover. I adored my brother and loved literature. Putting the two together in this narrative, as I did, made a creed out of literature and an idolater out of me. I still love *Go*, although I find it dark and maybe overwrought with feverish talk and rainy streets, and the young narrator terribly conscious of inadequacies and the depression they carry with them. But a faithful chronicle of an amazing time and people it will always be. So I love it, and even more perhaps I love having had the experience of reading it the first time and discovering how reality becomes coherent, so fragile, and yet so imperishable in the novelist's hands.

Well, I paraded *Go* to the cafeteria crowd, warning them of the fine novel that this brother they joked about had made and that would come out and astound them all. But that would be much later and after much water had flowed under many bridges as my own world moved inexorably from the inchoate innocence of knowledge-gathering—sufficient in itself—to the guilt of living. By the time John's book came out in September 1952, during my junior year in college with all the advanced courses in history and English, living was intruding more and more on learning. The sad taint of experience and its subtle corruptions of the heart were creeping in.

My twentieth year—John gave me one of the first copies of his book, inscribed,

> "October 1, 1952
> For Liz—who was one of the very first to read and appreciate it—my love—
>
> > John"

On the fly leaf it says,

> "Clellon Holmes——*Go*, 1952
> Charles Scribner's Sons
> New York"

Ah, time.

Chapter 7

Breakup at 4C

———— Sometime in the previous year, after John had gotten his advance for *Go*—my memory becomes blank here for exact dates and even years—John came upstairs and told us that he and Marian were splitting up. No, this was not a date in a year for me—it marked a wounding of my soul. I sat shocked in a first death of the heart as he talked cold practicality with my mother. They had agreed, he and Marian, that he would move out, that she would stay in 4C and he would give her half his advance money. She had a decent job now as secretary to Erwin Piscator of the City College Film Institute. I knew she was meeting all kinds of people, like Harry Belafonte and Tony Curtis ("Bernie Schwartz," she sniffed.) She had made herself indispensable to the famous German director, so she would stay on. I sat on and on hearing all this in my dead swoon on the couch. Then John got up to go—nothing more to say—and looked at me. "I'm sorry, Liz. These things happen. We tried the best we could."

Another time they both came up—there is no sequence in my time line for these events, nothing like "this happened when that was going on while Jack was on the road and I was taking Shakespeare," like the charts on the bottom of the pages of histories. No, some events rise up like boulders blasting the others out of the stream. Instead of a series of rapids joggling along on the surface, the water free falls a thousand feet over the cliff. "Yes," I said to Mom, "they always seemed to try so hard. All that trying." And I went in my room and played Parker loud so that she wouldn't hear me bawl.

The tectonic plates of my planet of 681 had shifted, and I felt the awful grinding and wounding as I lay on my cot. For the first time in my little life, the sweetness of music failed to put me to sleep. The lights of apartments and the neon city sky bathed my room in their tarnish as I lay in my new black hole of grief. I had hardly noticed the breakup of my parents, my father having lived apart from us since I could remember, and my sister's breakup with her first husband had happened in California, way off my stage, and she had visited us only once in a while with Don. I kind of liked him, but their split didn't matter anyway since Lila had been marginal in my life.

But the earth revolved around John and Marian, and it quaked and ripped asunder with their split. They were the couple who quarreled over money and work troubles and pulled at each other out of their frustrations, but who together were my reality bedrock like the black granite of Manhattan that anchored the giddy top-heavy skyscrapers and kept them from falling. This breakup was terrible, and most horrible was the certain knowledge that it had nothing to do with me. I was not being abandoned, they didn't *not* love me as you're supposed to feel when Mom and Dad divorce. I was too old to indulge that egoism. The reason for their breakup was all out there in the winds of a witless chaos, and I was reduced to helpless sobs that died away inside that wind. After all, hadn't they clung together in the conclusion of *Go*, her head nestling into his chest on the ferry coming home from Hoboken after the horror of Cannastra's death, for the moment grafted to each other like Siamese twins as he searched north of the Chrysler Building for 681? *Go* was literature, and wasn't that for all time? Now here came this grave, nauseating split corrupting the image forever. I was silent, distraught, and entombed in the first of life's dumps.

Later, they did come up together and put on a beautiful heart-lifting act for me. They were so good—trying again, only now out of their new relationship—that I almost let go of the tears I had shown no one so far.

"Don't worry, honey," Marian said, standing by Mom's dresser where the roaches came out and partied in the evening. "I'll still be downstairs. And Johnny won't be far. We still love each other. We just have to live apart for a while. You'll be okay. We still love you."

"Yes, Liz," John said, standing too, as they couldn't stay long and had business to attend to. "I won't be far. Marian and I are still friends. I'll be in the city. Things'll go on—maybe not exactly the same, but not *that* different. You know, marriages break up, and often it's for the best for everyone."

I wanted to cry for them with all this blather coming out just for me. I knew marriages broke up—Mom, Dad, Lila, Jack. But, of course, John and Marian had been different. I had never thought of them in those ordinary terms. Now I felt sorry for them. It seemed, after all, that I had no right to make people different in such ways. It was terrifying and sickening with taint and corruption, and it was all in my head. They had tried hard—and that saved them in my mind for me as I had been a silent witness to their efforts—but they hadn't made it. That, of course, was the fruit of the tree of life. Their divorce was the first bitter taste of that fruit for me.

Their love for me had also made them play-act for me because they had gone through a nasty split with ugly meetings in lawyers' offices, mean attacks over money—bitterness, jealousy, rages, and hate. All of it came out and was reported in disjointed talks with Mom in 5D. John didn't come often, but he did check in with increasing anger and cold tales. Oh, he didn't want me to get mad at Marian, but *he* sure was, wanting openly to be finished with her and to get this "damned fucking thing over with!" Then it slowly came out that he had a new girl and was in love with her and nothing was going to stop them, though Marian was "making everything pure hell!" Marian came up too, but not often. She seemed to be holding tight to herself, was hurt and tender with me, but mad at John and quietly sarcastic about him to my mother. "You, know, Betty, how he just still hasn't grown up—always playing at life, all the parties and crazy people—and now, going off in a romantic dither." She'd tap her cigarette crisply as her crossed leg jerked up and down, her little musclely calf angry in its stocking. "I'm pretty fed up with it, Betty." Deep, night-brown circles under eyes, bitter sniffle, eyes black with pain striking out against her will. "But anyway, you know it doesn't affect my feelings for you and Liz. I love you both. Come down and visit sometime, Liz."

So the plates shifted and ground the edges jagged and raw. Effects: John only came up with bare, grinding reports on personal catastrophe interspersed with the ongoing success of book-processing. Failure and success pulled him along on their own autonomous roads. There were no more excited tales of prophetic, original people and the revelations they had flooded him with. Neal was gone, Jack was gone, Allen Ginsberg was gone or going. Alan Harrington, who had moved next door in 5C with his wife, Virginia, and their baby, Steve, was leaving them for his lady friend, Marya, and they would move to upper Madison, and Virginia would lie in bed with TB coughing her life away until her rich father put her in a sanatorium in Connecticut, and 5C would stand empty.

My mother had also decided to move, this time to Old Saybrook, Connecticut. For years, she had yearned to leave New York. Hadn't I paid attention to all her failed ventures in escape? To Arizona one summer where she couldn't follow through on the smallest payment for the pretty meadowland she hankered after. Another summer in the Berkshires where a crafty German war survivor inveigled her into a partnership for an inn, then nosed her out with a third mortgage when she had no more to give. But now she was really going. An inheritance had come through for her, so she could get her furniture out of storage at last. She could leave the two-bit jobs and dinners at Joe's and the roaches on her dresser and move into an old Victorian. And, alas, John himself with more of that *Go* money could help her buy the land and the house in the back for himself and his new girlfriend, Shirley Allen, who was sparring violently with her own madman husband, Stanley Radulovich. They would all eventually and finally leave the emerald isle of Manhattan that had for them become a hellhole of rancor and mayhem and bitterness—and they could all say, "To hell with it!" and that was that.

Actually there had been early signs of darkness up ahead—tea leaves that I hadn't known how to read but had tasted bitter anyway. A year or so before all this family calamity and upheaval, Bill Cannastra, the demiurge of Manhattan, stuck his head out a subway window as it entered the tunnel; his neck was snapped and he was dead—crack, poof, gone—a simple clean act of destruction. I had never seen the man—only in nightmare reverie. A haunting he had been. Now he was more real than the person sitting next to me on the IRT, and I stared at the small generic window at the front of the car that he had opened for his consummation. For a month it seemed that he had opened every window on every subway car I rode. Even now I'll catch myself recreating that specter in the new cars with their sterile lighting and dead voice-overs, "Next stop, Astor Place . . ." He reared up for me in the live legend of death—the true demiurge of our town, our own daemon from hell. John was a compelling storyteller, and he had conjured up a world for me that held the secret life of my adolescence. This Cannastra-self-immolation had probably been the first sign of its dissolution.

There had been other minor off-notes as well. One night during our jolly times at Birdland, Howie and I had wandered back to the glassed-in studio where Symphony Sid did his radio show that accompanied all the wild hijinks of the city. A merry crowd of young hipsters usually goofed around in front of the glass cheering him on. He had a paunchy fallen face, gray greasy hair, hills of flesh under his eyes—just the look that the grouchy voice that comforted us through the night demanded. The corrupt voice and the pure bop sounds he purveyed, with never a slip into the corny or sentimental, was a magical nocturnal combination. He saved many a discordant night for a lot of us in those days. So we goofed around laughing, clapping, and yelling "Go!" into his glassed-in silence. He turned the records, took long wet drags on his cigarette, and mostly ignored our commotion. On this particular night, he went through his spiel, got the record going, and lit the cigarette with beefy yellow fingers. Then he looked up, I swear, right at Howie and me, and with end-of-the-world eyes, put his cigarette down and reached up with both hands, dislodged his upper teeth, and waved them at us. "God," I thought, "how much he really hates us!" We all turned away and straggled back to our chairs, feeling like the bleacher-bums we were. There, already in late 1949 and 1950, a little taint was creeping in to drop through the cracks.

Life doesn't stand aside forever. In the fall of 1952, it came in rollicking and roaring, declaring its stamp of chaos, as if to say, "Enough of this happy learning, this joyful secondhand knowledge of the possibilities of beauty and harmony in art and life. You're on the track now—on your own with all the pitfalls and minefields you'll have to struggle with for the duration, pretty Miss Missy. Now, go!" Whew! I was overwhelmed that fall of 1952, every escape-block falling into place for all of them. Here they were all lined up: at Marian's urging John writes the book that will be accepted by Scribner's who will give him the advance that will enable him to give her half which will help him leave her, while Mom's inheritance will materialize simultaneously, and together she and John will be able to buy the compound in Old Saybrook and the inexorable move to that town at the mouth of the Connecticut River will begin. It could have seemed like a paranoiac conspiracy to me, but it was not—just life gathering together its forces to execute our several fates.

John left Marian and 681 Lexington and moved to a seventh floor walk-up on Forty-ninth Street and Second Avenue. It had a large kitchen with a bathtub and water closet off to the side, a small living room already lined with homebuilt bookshelves with records and a phonograph fitting snugly in a lower shelf, one window in a far corner, and the usual shadowy bedroom with its nocturnal light from a dark window. I was to camp there many times, and even took a friend there once in a while. But most of the time, I would be there alone in the afternoon, rarely seeing John since he would be with Shirley fighting their guerilla wars with their respective embittered mates. Or he would escape to Saybrook, where my mother now lived, leaving behind the battlefields of New York.

Alan Harrington and his wife Virginia had gone their separate ways, it seemed to my new tragic eyes, just before Virginia coughed her last. A friend of theirs, Alex Eliot, who wrote about art for *Time*,

had been coming to our door asking about her, and with a forlorn
face, leaving flowers for her—too afraid, I gathered, to enter the
house of death. God, I thought, she is truly dying right on the other
side of the wall in 5C. The summer before, I had walked with her
and Steve to the zoo in Central Park where we had gazed for hours
at the seals. Now she hacked on and on until everybody wanted to
scream and run from the horror of her. Alan had gone with Marya,
baby Steve was taken by a family member. We were all going crazy
until her father came into the mess of the derelict, dying apartment where she lay on the couch amid aisles of books, papers, and
clothes—and scooped her up from the debris of her 681 life where
Alan had chased cockroaches with shoe in hand to the windowsill
where they would leap off the fifth floor before the shoe came down
and "move busily into the next building without a care. Miraculous beings, the little bastards!" he'd say. No wonder he wrote about
Merko, the human fly. So now Virginia, with her hacking death call,
was safely in her own Connecticut sanatorium.

Of course, Marian was downstairs in 4C, but our tie had become
inexorably tenuous. She checked on me dutifully, and there was still
the innate warmth of her Marian-being, but she was cool with a tiny
edge of shortness to her manner. Still her smile would creep up to
the side against her will, and I would burble tears inside wanting to
hug her, but that was gone now, replaced by little good-bye pecks
with hands on arms, paltry leftovers of early love-years.

One evening she asked me to come down to 4C. She usually
called me on the phone in those days. I went in—how mournful the
old room felt in the autumn gloom of six o'clock, the same couches
and tables, but the bookcases gone, their shelves now reassembled on
Forty-ninth Street, only one little case of books that she'd kept and
a phonograph with an operatic voice soaring into the emptiness.
A truly huge man with a broad, kind, virile face sat on the couch
where Jack had cradled his girlfriends.

"Liz, this is Yael. He's in film at the institute. We're having some
wine. Join us for a glass."

Yael was casual and friendly, low-keyed like a Welsh uncle, appearing offhand and a bit curious about this ex-husband's sister. It was a quiet glass of wine. I was asked a few ordinary questions—about college, interests, the Village—and I talked like the twenty-year-old I was. A mournful, impersonal warmth moved between us here in 4C where there had been raucous outbursts, heavy talk about "our time," and gentle scenes of love all to the erratic beat of bop. I felt the old room crying over its losses—glooming and closing itself down away from me. I smiled, kissed Marian, and shook Yael's hand, thought how strong and attractive he was, and left. The next time I recall seeing him was a long time later when Marian had left 681 and moved with Yael to Greenwich Village and I stopped after classes to have another glass of wine amid the distracted happy bustle of their new life.

Much water had passed under all their bridges by that time and I had a new "sister-in-law" whose own apartment at 123 Lexington I would also camp in, either with Shirley Allen or alone, as at Forty-ninth Street when I needed to get away. Mom had kindly left our un-spayed Kitty with me for company when she left for Connecticut. So for the school year of 1952–53, Kitty and I stayed together, the last holdouts up in 5D under the skylight among the new strangers of 681.

Chapter 8

Learning the Art of Moving On

—— The year that followed the leave-taking would be the year that all my people burrowed down into themselves and worked on their isolated destinies. There was nothing left for me but to challenge that year to be the first that I could call my own. And so I did.

I still tried to trade on John, the brother who was largely absent now but who still sought my appreciation in a new, more personal direction. I gleamed around the cafeteria when his Beat article came out in *The New York Times*. "See," my high head said to all my friends, "See how important he is." I was still a kid, incredulous over any dispassionate critique of his prophetic words, and the critiques came—some puffing and snorting about overwrought rhetoric, flimsy generalizations, mountain-out-of-molehill arguments—mostly to get my gall. But I took it, acted smug, and clung inside to the old idol of the apocalyptic tales and legendary heroes. In those months, I was getting the first of many lessons in that hateful skill that kills the tender past: the art of "moving on." My own fragile heart that held Kitty in my lap would not learn it well, and, in fact, would resist it in devious ways.

I went to my classes, studied and performed well, talked, joked, drank with my friends, went on dates with a black trumpet player from Queens—Roy II, a friend of my first black lover, Roy from Staten Island. He toured with a band, had money, and took me to Birdland where we sat at a table, had our picture taken, and I met

Lester Young, who slid by all loose and musing with "Hey, man" and a hand on Roy's shoulder. He took me to chrome-plated Italian mob restaurants on Broadway where he knew the waiters and they gave me special pastel drinks decorated with fruit and striped swizzle sticks. And he took me to an intimate high-end jazz club, Le Downbeat, located way west by Eighth Avenue and some dark midtown street. Time after time we went there, with Billy Taylor and Milt Jackson and Howard McGhee on the little stand in the back and where the more sophisticated jazz DJ, Billy Williams, could be seen with his date, Ava Gardner, sitting in the small balcony—until the night when we stood at the bar waiting for a table and some angry white goofballs charged in and grabbed Roy, dragged him out, and threw him around the sidewalk and into a parking sign. The bouncer got the cab and shoved us in before they killed him—or as he reached into his vest pocket, pulling out only an empty hand to flip at them. "Goddamn," he said, with a bruised head on my shoulder, "that's the first time I've been out with you without my gun!" I trembled in my innocence, swimming out of my depth in complex racial waters. Roy was such a kind, cryptic young man who never pushed the sex thing to the finish because I didn't love him and I was being celibate those years. With his reticence and his gun, he was a good caregiver and I was lonely—more so than I knew.

Yes, in the apartment where there had once been heady talk and family members gathering to go to Joe's for dinner and Jack listening to Red Moscow with me and Neal digging me dig Wardell Gray and Mom with WQXR[13] and John and Marian sparring over a coming party—here I went to sleep at night with yellow Kitty on the edge of Mom's cot, alone in a way that would take its toll, life inexorably moving in its new directions.

A brown, lonesome November in 1952. I see myself sitting on John's couch at Forty-ninth Street. There is an extra pack of Chesterfields on the table in front of me. I don't want to have to go down seven flights in the middle of the night, desperate for smokes. I want to stay the night here, and you have to plan for emergencies

---

13. Editor's Note: WQXR was an AM station founded in New York in 1936, broadcasting mainly classical music recordings. WQXR-FM developed out of it in the late forties. It is now WQEW.

when you go to John's. He is gone, an absentee as he so often is this year. It is probably four o'clock in the afternoon. John has carefully shown me how to use the phonograph and the exact arrangement of his records—the placement of the Parkers, Miles Davis' *Birth of the Cool* sides, the Stan Getz Four Brothers. Right now I'm putting on Thelonius Monk's "'Round Midnight." I sit and smoke, pensive but without thoughts in the gloomy comfort of his walls of books; John always lives within thick, nocturnal walls of books, so that even when gone he assures me of his presence. I sit and smoke, Monk's dirge calling me to look out the spy hole of the gray window in the corner. Across a well of air, the tall buildings of Tudor City lift themselves beyond my sight. There must be a mist. I see their walls stained with moisture below the windows as though they are lamenting some hidden and monumental grief. The great city hulks remain anchored in rock, unable to move, lonesome at the fall of another day. Monk's notes are so suggestive and with the window that only delivers twilight, even on a sunny morning, I become physically and impersonally sad. Who am I, after all, when the stained yellow bricks of New York are even sadder? Though I didn't know why I wanted to hole up here with John's books and records, it had worked. It was delicious to float away on a Monk/Manhattan melancholy mood. If you could still yourself—escape your personal frets—loneliness itself could flood you with strange, beautiful regret.

I played the record for a half hour until the mood did its job and I was able to work on a term paper. John said that Monk rarely left New York and lived with his mother uptown someplace. I ached with love for New York now, rising up out there and dripping with all its losses—all the people, all the jobs, all the parties—just passing through and always leaving, moving on. All these apartments—4C, Tudor City, this seventh floor walk-up, all filled with the accumulations of binges, loves, tears, too much life lived and lost to hold without scarring its bricks with melancholy. Poor place—doomed always to loss.

So I was lonely, although I didn't say so to myself, and here there were always people filling my days. Before long I met John's new girl-friend Shirley. In a strange way, John seemed to push and prepare me for this meeting. I counted now, as if I were all of what was left. "I want you to meet Shirley, Liz. She's smart and sharp and digs everything, and I know you'll like her. She's very important to me and you're my sister and you two must like each other. She's anxious to meet you."

And we did. At a very precise hour, John took me for drinks at the Inkspot, a press bar located somewhere in the east forties near her job, this apparently their own private love-bar. I don't remember where we sat, although I see her at the bar, her smartly crossed legs barely touching the rung, and a cigarette in her upraised hand. Her hair was brown and pulled back; her face was broad with wide eyes and mouth etched tight on its fair skin. Her mouth, drawn finely in red, spread flat in a winning smile. "How pretty she is with her brown eyes—so merry and knowing," I thought. Not an easy catch for John's sister; Shirley would take a long slow study—no quick embraces and effusions—and she would be worth it. We sat and we drank (I still settled on beer most of the time.) and we chatted the usual.

But what we really did was work the jukebox. "I hear you really like jazz, honey?" She had southern ways. "Looosiana Cajun," she said, and was ready with verbal caresses. But they weren't soft and lush. No, they came out warm with gritty edges—all these "honeys." She got up—my God, another miniature dynamo! John and his petite women—all five feet of her, and went to the jukebox. "Listen to this Peggy Lee 'Lover,' honey—and DIG!" It was a steam engine that rolled up and up until you couldn't stand it anymore—"Lover, lover, LOVER!" We girls laughed and cried and stomped together as John looked pleased and moved his head back and forth. We played the record over and over for an hour. Then we went our separate ways for the evening. We kissed or shook hands—I don't know which. Music-sisters for a start. Not bad.

There was continuity, too, during that period. I began to notice mini-Beat groups here and there. There was a bunch of young fellows in the cafeteria who ran an unofficial literary magazine, who acted like the next generation of Beat writers. One was a hulky blond boy with thick lips and thicker glasses, sensitive and inarticulate in the Jack Kerouac mold, who slouched around the tables. He lived in

New Rochelle and wrote stories. But mostly he paid homage to
the hero of the group, a jittery, wiry fellow with a mat of tight hair
and eyes close together and maniacal with energy—yes, like Neal
Cassady. And by God, if he wasn't from Denver too! He camped in
the huge seedy Broadway Central Hotel where certain homeless
NYU students rented cheap rooms. I knew a fellow, a gay boy in
my English class, who lived there and said that, yes, true to form, the
Beat guys' parties shook the place and that the Neal-type was always
being thrown out only to wheedle his way back in with Neal-cons.
They were a clubby group, pretty much ignoring the rest of us, so
arrogant they were about carrying on the Beat message. Yes, John
had really been on to something, or else he was insinuating something that young guys were in the mood to ape slavishly. And this
was even before *On The Road* surfaced—1953! It seemed that Beat
legends filled the city air, so that if you looked carefully you could
find mini-Neals and Jacks and Ginsbergs all over the place. I watched
their occult antics from afar, even fancied the slouching Tom/Jack
one. But for the most part they wearied me—so self-conscious they
were, in a way the originals had never been.

A friend of mine in Shakespeare class was part of another small
clique. Benny and his girl, Bea, were rosy-cheeked, bright, hard-work-
ing students. He was chubby with clear eyes and oddly fresh cheeks—
as if he hadn't shaved yet—and tight blond hair, which increased the
effect of sunniness he projected. Benny was brilliant in an easygo-
ing friendly way, not with one-liners but rather the wit of trenchant,
funny remarks that didn't demand a witty response. We got along, and
soon I was going to their apartment in the west forties between Fifth
and Sixth, the usual slanty-staired, dreary, one-bedroom place with
soot-filtered light peeking through the streaked windows.

Benny had a tall friend, Klute, with a mustache and marvelous
buck teeth that registered irrepressible humor. I soon learned that
teeth like Klute's fostered sad sack self-deprecation that had you on
the floor laughing until you peed your pants. He prated on about his
forlornness, his bent-over skinniness, his inadequacies, his sexlessness,
his friendless life. I began to hang around with him and remember
one day sitting at his kitchen table in the cold-water flat. His phone

was on the wall and he was lamenting in overdrive about its never ringing. For years he never heard it until he was desperate to use it himself. Then he fell off his chair and began scrabbling at his wall that was filled with phone numbers. "My numbers, my numbers!" he yelled, choking and gasping for the numbers to save him. He was a hoot. He had a buddy in the army who would sneak in AWOL from New Jersey to rustle up tea for them. Benny proclaimed them both really wild and "gone!"

Benny, with a bourgeois intellectual's predilection for the wild side, had read *Go* and John's *New York Times* article and swore that his gang was the real thing. I was getting the point that Beat now meant mildly aberrant and very funny to some young men around campuses. I liked Benny and his few cohorts and actually invited them up to Saybrook once for a weekend party where Benny was genuinely thrilled to meet and talk with the revered chronicler of the amazing Beat generation. He was not intimidated and met John on an open and admiring footing—equal, but respectful. For an intellectual and a smart one too, Benny was so full of good humor. Poor Benny. After they left, John said how likeable Benny was and "so square."

Oh well. In the winter of 1953, I introduced John and Shirley to a fellow that John would take very seriously indeed, a man of devotion who would soon sacrifice himself in the public marketplace. This was Gene Sharp, introduced to me by Hugh, another black friend of mine on campus. Gene was his friend and idol, a strange and radiant young fellow who lived in a marginal section of Brooklyn. In Gene, I saw a gaunt, tight skin-over-bones man with a youthful farm-fresh face and sibilant voice, a boy from Ohio living among the gangs of Brooklyn. He was lovely but ineffable somehow—untouchable, though he took my hand in both of his and kissed me on the cheek—"Under the mistletoe," he pointed up over his door. "Everyone enters this door with a kiss," he laughed.

In fact, Gene giggled over silly things and made small talk like the rest of us. But he was *not* like the rest of us—not at all. He lived under a wall poster of Gandhi and wrote pamphlets and later books on non-violent movements to gain all ends (economic, political, social), to roil up all social functioning. He was serious at a deep level where most of us are a mush of confusion. It was as though at the center of his body, the solar plexus behind the navel, there lived a coil of steel that was nondegradable, that would carry him to a firing squad if that were called for: Where our middles would quaver and fall, Gene's would stand. It held him so steadily that on the surface he was light and free—giggling, sibilant, flitting through his rooms (another cold water flat) whimsical, effeminate. I loved him, though he was never too grave with me, just careful, feeding me good legume stews and Indian rices and walking me through the streets on and on one night when I thought I'd drunk too much—holding my arm tight, walking the sickness out of me. John took Gene very seriously. He was in an Indian/Gandhian phase and talked the fervent depths of conviction to him for what must have been hours. He and Shirley began visiting Gene on their own at times, John in an odd fit of admiration for Gene, although he argued and pressed realities with him.

It was clear to all of us during that spring of 1953 that Gene was heading toward his consummation. He was called to the draft but refused to register. His court date was coming and some of his friends went to the courthouse in Brooklyn to witness for him. He spoke his piece in a low sibilant voice, strong enough to resonate in the high room. The judge might have thought he was gay, but he knew, as we all did, that that was beside the point. What kind of love and tender succor he gave to the young toughs of his neighborhood was his own business. They never refused his love. Here the judge was forced up to Gene's dispassionate ground and gave him two years in the Federal Correctional Institute in Danbury, Connecticut.

I heard that he was allowed two correspondents, and for some reason it sticks in my mind that he chose his mother and John. I kissed him good-bye in the courtroom and have since then watched him from afar become a steady light of scholarship and devotion to a beleaguered cause. He lives now in Boston, directing his own institute for non-violent resistance to oppression. I was not sorry he chose John to write to. Beneath my awareness, they had cemented a friendship.

Chapter 9

Falling Down to Beatness

—— That was a bad spring for me. I was not cementing anything but a novel and perilous bond with booze. It all began that winter when a graduate assistant in history, an older fellow in his thirties, loose-jointed, privately comic and so appealingly wise to my eyes, began coming into the cafeteria. I wonder now, if out of his own idiosyncratic isolation, he wasn't scouting for a drinking partner. At the time, we were both vaguely marginal, sitting on the outskirts of a large shapeless group—assorted English and social science majors, people in film, a few philosophy and psychology types. We sprawled over four or five tables, mostly talking *beyond* each other. Bill Glass was bored and amused by it all, and, anyway, it was soon clear that he had more serious business to attend to. His face was saggy and sallow like fallen wax from a candle, and he always wore bulky unmatched tweed jackets and pants that he swayed around inside of. His eyes slitted up when he laughed, and his teeth were irregular and just beginning to tarnish. Like all of us, he smoked a lot, only he had done it a lot longer. And he drank a lot like some of us did, but very, very much more and harder and for a lot longer. So the things he did, while somewhat common to all of us, were beginning to leave their traces on him. And his wit, which some of us had, was subtler—

secret and refined like the gin he drank all afternoon and evening. Bill was pickled and aged in his habits, and he came across like the best of a single malt Scotch. I found him quite irresistible—attractive, urbane, different. He had never paid particular attention to me, but one afternoon he must have gotten the message sent by my curious face and appreciative laughter. "Will you have a drink?" he said.

Oh my. It was the most enticing offer I had had in years, if a twenty-year-old can think in such time. It was so personal, so directed to just *me* out of a crowd of some prettier, more brilliant girls, and yet not carried on the breath of sensual or romantic motive. Ah, yes, the drink was first, my particular company second but necessary.

In the sedate, twilit lounge of the Waverley Hotel, that drink—the perfumed, pale oil of a stand-up martini—was to last for the next four and then five, six, eight, and ten hours, three or four times a week through March, April, and May of 1953. It was wondrous and beautiful with all the easy sustenance of a long, slow swim when you reach the point where you know that to go on forever would take no more effort than the perfect rhythm of breath, arms, and legs that you have attained *now* in this exact moment. How many times did I feel during that spring that I had attained that balance, that easy rhythm? In the middle, it began at times to seem that we were floating free on just such a moment that extended into a carefree future. It was lovely.

Bill Glass was witty and kind and utterly without motive—just wanted to talk about history: "My dissertation, my dear, on the population of France in 1532—demographic analysis of a crucial kind"—department gossip, "I must uncover those pockets of faulty, obtuse scholarship in your idol, Professor Magnason"—his affair with a gloomy married Russian woman, "Yes, yes, tormented ecstasy à la Russe—soul-comes, the cunt, the chess, suicidal Russian games"— and lastly and lovingly, to talk about gin, "Lucky for me I don't drink with my prick!" I also talked—about Gene and non-violence, my brother, and the Beats. There was an easy give-and-take between us in these sessions. We held nothing back. Why should we? There was no consequence from exposure, for we had silently pledged with the first clink of glasses for the day not to give or ask anything of each other. Only and forever, it seemed, "the pleasure of our company."

I didn't know much about cocktail hour, only about beer binges and wild parties. But this new Bill was bringing me a step further into life—until life itself became one long cocktail hour. Oh, it was interrupted by a few hours of sleep (me in 681, Bill in a flat on East Fifth Street in the Bowery), a few classes, and even capricious and complicated adventures after four or five warm-ups. Bill and I would snake through the subway to Hoboken and River Street, the lowest circle of saloon-hell—from John's *Go*, I told him—where we made the bartender concoct martinis instead of the boiler-makers that he usually doled out—where, after Bill Cannastra's death, John and Marian had huddled together on the ferry as John looked for their home at 681 with the grave poetry of conclusion. Bill Glass and I swayed in the crashing tube and laughed down in Stalin's face in *The Daily News* on the floor—"STALIN DIES!"—continuing on to further martinis of nostalgia and celebration. Sometimes to sex films at the Pix on Forty-second Street, semen on the seats. We'd come out in the high spring sun of six o'clock with the exuberant realization that there were maybe eight more hours of martinis. "Amazing!" we felt in unison, "How absolutely good life is!"

I don't know if John and Shirley noticed, or Gene, or Roy, who still took me to the Broadway restaurants when he was in town, or my teachers and classmates. I don't know if *anybody* noticed. But I was an alcoholic for three months of spring 1953. I lived on gin after I discovered that it could lift you to an altitude where the strain of living, studying, and loving was suddenly relaxed. The seat belts were off, drinks were served—and I cruised. It was beautiful.

And then it was terrible. I sat alone one night in 5D, and the nerves began racing under my skin—an all-over running around over legs, arms—so hideous, the way it would feel if millions of roaches were crawling over the hills of my thighs in frantic, autonomous, purposeless activity, a fiendish business carrying my mind along with them to their little roach hell.

I felt a little better the next day—the roaches had calmed down, so I went to see Bill Glass, the only person who knew this me of May '53. But then walking down Fifth Street to his apartment, the horror happened. Every sensation hurt. Ash cans, women, and babies on stoops stabbed my eyes with binocular distortions, the cans and voices blared rackets inside my head, the fresh air from the river stung my nostrils, the lovely sun was an angry glare. All awful. All blasted into senselessness forever. All sense data spliced apart like the frames of a movie, each standing alone enlarged, frozen, incoherent. I just kept moving through it all, just as the denizens of hell must keep moving through their fires.

I felt better once I got inside the apartment, probably because it was the blackest, filthiest, most lovingly neglected apartment I had ever seen—a landscape of unsullied chaos where the details were strung together into a coherent theme of proud degradation. Bill Glass was a hero in his own right—it took guts, even a quirky love, to maintain equilibrium in a habitat that defied sanity in every detail. It took the affection of a perverse and minor god to create this habitat. The place breathed such occult wisdom, and I needed wisdom.

What I got was a mystery, at least to my feverish brain, which thirsted for nothing less than the meaning of life. "You're alone too much—come," he held me a while, then fixed me some gin, and gave me hair of the dog.[14] He gave me more and more, until I sat waiting an hour to be sick while he played chess by himself on the floor. Then I retched on and on. He smiled and cleaned up—all this gin turned rancid couldn't be neglected even here where neglect was an art. He walked me to the subway, as he had two and a half months earlier when all was promise like the buds on the trees in Washington Square, and he kissed me good-bye with the same kindness and lack of motive as he had then.

The cocktail hour was over, but the awfulness was not. Instead it had become a dull cancer on my psyche. It remained a bad late spring, and I worried about myself. A faceless gray spread over my thoughts and even over the sunny days of June. "Alone too much," Roy came and held my hand and said again, "Alone too much, kid,"

---

14. Editor's Note: An expression for the belief that the best cure for alcoholic poisoning is more alcohol, predicated on the folk wisdom that applying a few hairs of the dog that bit one to the wound itself will heal the wound.

and spent the night on the couch. Shirley said, "Come down to 123, Liz, you're probably alone too much." I started going to Saybrook on the weekends. "I don't know what's wrong, Mom, nothing makes much sense—it's all unhappy. Guess I'm a little lonely." Then going out to dinner with John and Shirley in Mom's old borrowed Packard, John asked me, "How's your reality, Liz?" I suppose I can say now that it was a Zen moment because something cracked in my head—a fissure opened in the gray maw and a little pinpoint of light smiled in—the first surprise in my thoughts for weeks now. "My reality," as though we all have our realities and they split apart at times—he said something like that—and then they slowly reassemble themselves as you just keep going through the motions, day after slogging day, until you are walking in your own rebuilt reality again. So going through the motions—I must take care as I begin these hangover days—I must move cautiously, must give study to their motions—the making of a bed, the rinsing out of stockings, the combing of hair, and the dusting off of a table. A new kind of attention must be paid when listening to a professor, talking to a friend, or offering a heart. John, I realized, was still a seer. After my first real bite of life, I needed him more than I ever had in the old palmy days when knowledge had brought only kicks in its coming.

By June, I amazingly had completed the school year with mostly As. And Bill Glass? He was going to spend the summer in the New York Public Library fleshing out the demographic bones of the population of France in 1532. (All I had seen in the elegant grime of his Fifth Street apartment had been those bones—tall wobbly stacks of index cards. Amazing those stacks were, standing their ground and even growing amidst turned-over glasses and drunken roaches puddling through the gin. His stacks had grown and my papers had been written while the gin had been drunk—up to ten a night—and my brain had been pickled and saw a world coated with martini oil and the blank stare of an olive-eye stuck in its middle.)

Postmortem effects—I had eighteen credits to go for the degree and had already registered for a three-hour Russian history course for the summer term, which would allow me to carry a normal fifteen-hour semester in the fall and get the BA in January 1954. I had to go fast. My father's patience about paying the tuition was wearing thin, especially as he assumed I would hook up with a guy and all this college stuff would go by the boards. A lot of money down the drain. "For what?" he asked my mother. And she could not go on paying the rent on 5D forever. Of course, Bill Glass had taken care of most of the food—a hamburger before the Waverley, another one sometime during the night.

With my head cracking up and my "reality" still reeling with hangover, I sat in 5D and stared the summer of 1953 in the face. Ah, summer with the open skylight and two windows like gashes sending oven heat into the apartment, with soot blackening every wounded surface, and the cockroaches out in the daylight, shamelessly vacationing on all their favorite spots—dresser, tub, card table, living room cot. Oh, oh, oh, with poor Kitty yowling, her fur coming out in knots, her mouth open in a pant and her back-end up in hopeless lust, the tenant downstairs banging on the radiator as my latest Bird and Diz screech out through the useless window, and the mustachioed man sitting in his boxers reading the paper before going to the john where he doesn't bother to close the window or the shade as he makes love to himself. Would the study of Ivan the Terrible and the Boyars sweeten the horror flick I saw before me? Alone too much. Alone too much. Alone, Alone. The summer of 1953 was a devil making right for me. Clearly, I had to run.

"Mom, I'm coming up there for the summer. It's so hot and empty here and I'm only taking one course. What'll I do with myself? Anyway, I can handle eighteen hours in the fall. I'll come up this weekend with my stuff. It'll be nice up there. I can swim and help you with the big garden you want. Didn't you talk about a whole line of gladiolus around the backyard? And the inn you're going to start—all those rooms on the third floor? I can help with the beds. Maybe I can find a summer job up there? So, can you come down and get me and Kitty in the old Packard? It'll be better for her, maybe she'll go out and sit in the sun . . ." and on and on, working up this sunlit paradise of escape—blabbing on to myself about this jolly, healthy summer and how Old Saybrook was my promised land, blabbing on to her until I persuaded myself of my new-won wisdom in choosing to leave 681 that summer—*now*—without delay. All the while I was trembling and wringing my psychic hands and running hard from 681 visions. Talk, talk, reason to old Mom—and wail inside. Truth was, I couldn't think beyond August. September was an oblivion to my inner eye. The fall return to 681 with its known and maybe unknown and terrifying apparitions shut off my brain. This looming summer of '53 was my only future.

My mother, true to her sit-down, placid, solitaire-playing, trust-in-what-is self, said, "Yes, Liz dear, I think it would be good for you to get out of the city." She bought all my devious reasoning, even though she suspected there was a fly in this happy ointment—swim, summer, sun bathe, garden—then jump back into the bottomless well of solitude in September? So she came down, or somebody drove her down to the mysterious car-world of Manhattan, and they picked me up with my one twelve-pocket record album (Oh, horror! What wrenching choices.), my one bag, Kitty and her little accoutrements (two little bowls and some newspapers—there wasn't much litter then, or at least we didn't know of such an amenity, and laid papers down for her in the bathroom where the long-haired nervous beauty lowered her sad overworked backside down to pee among the roaches). Poor Kitty. She wasn't desperate and fleeing like her mistress. She lolled on the floor in the heat, her yellow fur fell off her in knots, she shat amongst the roaches, and she howled for her lost mate and lived her life anywhere. Oh, but she would be better in Saybrook, I knew, though she didn't set her life by such standards. So she shivered and keened with a new strange torture of the car ride, and we went up the old Merritt Parkway and then over a sylvan country road to the Big Victorian, Main Street, Old Saybrook.

Two days later, Monday morning, I took my bag and a paper sack with the record album in it, and Mom drove me to the station to catch the morning train to Grand Central. During that time, Kitty had come out of hiding and was dropping her knots on Mom's threadbare rugs and sniffing the air in the windows. She would be fine, at least for a while. I would go back up the five flights to 5D, to no-holes-barred, throbbing-skylight, locked-door solitary. No way out this time. My own Sunday choice had condemned me to all-out summer isolation.

But there in my little room was the narrow cot with the blue cover, the portable record player on the table next to it and the full line of albums in a row beneath, any one of which I could play right now, and then the poor mustachioed man in his boxers would be sad and beautiful like everything else. Only *here* in my shabby, forlorn, waiting home was I a sorcerer who could make paradise right now, right here—at 681 Lexington.

I don't think that it was music that brought me back that Monday, although I can't be sure. But it was music that said "Yes!" to my homecoming and buoyed up my choice until it was strong enough to face the old ghosts of New York. "Yes!" said Bud Powell in "Tea For Two"; "Yes!" from Monk with "Lulu's Back in Town"; "Yes!" from Bird in "Scrapple From the Apple," "Donna Lee," "Now's The Time," and "Sippin' At Bells"; "Yes!" in "Move" and "Jeru" from Miles; "Yes!" from Lester with "Just You, Just Me" and Prado with "More Mambo Jambo"; and after a couple of hours, the final "Yes!" from Wardell as he swung me through "Groovin' High."

Well, hadn't I come through my own "dark night of the soul" that John and Jack had always gone on about—sloshing through the springtime in a river of martinis until I woke up to a world swirling to an end in reality-hangover? Hadn't I tasted the bitter dregs of the morning-after end-game void? Hadn't I pushed through the sunny Saybrook morning of headache to find my way back to the poor old Manhattan scene of the crime, to play the music and feel the battered soul of me raw, ready and, at last, beat? I opened the window to let in the soft breeze of hot soot and whistled with Wardell out across the airshaft and the pulsing watery tar roof to the open windows of the self-lover's apartment house and was happy, almost as happy as I'd been on that January day, 1947, six years before, when I first stepped into 5D.

Chapter 10

The "Russian" Summer of 1953

——— Almost like that, but not quite. Let's backtrack. The weekend in Saybrook had been bright and beautiful. The clouds fluffed overhead in a cerulean sky not yet hazed by summer blare, and the breeze came gently over the fens from the Sound where I swam in light cool water on Saturday afternoon. We had a swordfish dinner at a river inn in Old Lyme. Mom's own inn was taking shape on the third floor of her huge calm Victorian house with book room and music room (including an old pump organ and square piano) and matching fireplaces and study with rolltop desk and wide kitchen with five-foot round oak table, and her plants in every room and in all the halls up and down, in every corner, by every window—hundreds of plants that must have sprouted out of a burst-open Mom-heart that had throbbed shut-up in cockroach heaven in 5D. I watched her for a full half hour as she watered every one, everywhere.

But the inn was a family project. John and Shirley talked to me on the run through a bustle of buckets and paint brushes and *only* about the small rooms on the third floor they were turning into Dickensian guest chambers—each named after one of his novels—an *Oliver Twist*, a *Nicholas Nickleby*, a *Little Dorrit*, *David Copperfield*, *Dombey and Son*, and even *Martin Chuzzlewit*—six in all. "Guess we can't

have *Bleak House* or *Hard Times*. Too bad, they're two of his best."
"Maybe the bathroom, hey, hon, for *Hard Times!*" said Shirley, with a
white splotch on her pert nose. All the rooms were whitewashed and
furnished with high-spool double beds, commodes with bowls and
pitchers on them, and appropriate, finely calligraphied nameplates
made by Shirley, who did charming floral still lifes of flowers tumbling out of wide bowls with dancing lines. She had studied art at
Washington University in St. Louis and had even been taught a little
by Max Beckman. Mom arranged flowers in all the rooms—opulent
bunches of daffodils, lilacs, and wisteria from her arbor outside the
kitchen. The perfume through the house made you reel and swoon.
They were all in a happy dither of activity and enterprise.

I couldn't find my way in all the commotion. Where was the
thread of continuity that tied all this Victorian domestic idyll with
the rented, rootless hip life in bars, at parties, of bop, books, and beatness? I felt lost at sea between New York roaches and English pastoral. I was not at home. Everyone welcomed me, but didn't know
what to do with me. John and Shirley had put their own stamp
on the remodeling. Mom was nowhere near ready for her gladiola
project—the lawn was still all grass. The town was too strange to
look for a job—not something I was ever eager to do anyway, still
clinging as I did to the old tree of knowledge way of innocence. Jobs
smelled too much of the *laws* of life—rules, repetition, the world
forcing your tender nose to its grindstone and the only reward the
dead dry smell of money. Oh, oh, work—the numbing of the mind,
the corrosion of the hopeful heart.

So I could swim all day and go to dinner at quaint Connecticut
inns where the talk was all about the accessories for the Chuzzlewit
room, then to bed with one of the twelve records on the creaking
leftover turntable, maybe the first one John gave me in the summer
of '46, and by August, sing with Billie about "Easy Living" for the
fiftieth time to bring on sleep.

By Sunday morning Saybrook had done its job. Now everything
about New York made sense—the three hours of Russian history, the
paid-for apartment lived in as it should be, the road toward the degree

taken up again. Now a hundred miles away, New York suddenly held
the magic again—the maelstrom, the elixir—goddamn it, the waters
of youth! In a weekend my sore head had cleared, the martini-film
that had clouded my sight until the reality it saw split into discon-
nected pieces that swooshed chaos into my head had sunk away in
the zephyrs coming from the Sound. It was all so lovely and ineffable here and how gently it told me that I was far from having
the pastoral heart. Instead of collapsing in a swoon of easy living, I
had become hard and bright and strong and found solace in a new
toughened heart that even looked forward to complete 5D solitary
now without dear knotty Kitty. She had found her place here—as
had Mom and John and Shirley.

Well, maybe your place was where your strengths led you. Something was arguing me back to 681, and I could only hope it was a
strength that had surfaced out of chaos and hangover. I would probably need it for 5D—with fifth floor wet-oven heat, its little world
coated in soot, the open gashes of windows that spewed out summer
hysterics, everybody's radios, yells, laughter, rages too loud, indifferent,
anti-social, or everybody else lounging with breasts hanging out and
open boxers in front of window fans. With nobody caring anymore
in the still un-air-conditioned city. With the falling off of companions—Bill Glass in the library and surely replacing me for his cocktail
hour, Gene in jail and not writing to me, Marian off with Yael to the
Westchester of her heart for vacation, Roy II on tour, Benny and
Bea married and burrowing into intimacy—my old cafeteria buddies spread out in summer lostness, Forty-ninth Street abandoned as
John was coming more and more into his own pastoral heart. Shirley
in a Victorian hiatus between jobs, leaving her own 123 Lexington
a summer derelict—though they still kept it, a vestigial remain that
I would occasionally swelter, fester, and languish in. Their hearts had
moved into escape mode, and it was clear without ambiguity that
they had *earned* escape. It was *their* current strength, as it was my
current weakness. And it would lead them to marriage in the fall.
Marriage against many odds must arrive out of a weird unrealized
strength that startles its bearers into action.

And so I announced, "Mom, I've got to go back to New York. I've registered for the course and I'm going to take it. Then I'll have a good and really easy fall semester. I'm on the top of my game now with college and taking only what I love. So I'm going back. In fact, I'm ready this afternoon." But no, I had missed the last Sunday train—frustrating. I was suddenly so eager. I felt so strong, ticking off all the city horrors to myself. How funny and exciting they were! So strong and without a clue as to why or where it came from—this novel, stalwart heart—only that it made me happy. It was enough.

★ ★ ★ ★

Once back at 681, I lay down on the blue cot, stripped to my underpants. Who cared? The backsides of all the buildings around the concrete pad with the tree of heaven flapping its grimy leaf-wings in our open gashes, showed the half- and all-naked bodies in equal languid sprawl. Across the fire escape in 5E was skinny, brown Mrs. Accolina, her breasts tiny wrinkled mounds on bone ridges and her tummy sunken in at the belly button, rocking a sweaty two-year-old, his bottom a shiny blob hanging over her done-in arm. She stuck her pelvis out to catch the stray whiff of breeze on her pubic hair—a black wiry mat in the open window, hoping for surcease of its swelter. I had often babysat for her two kids and would take them this summer to the river at Fifty-seventh Street so that she could stop, splay her worn-down flesh out on the sheets, and breathe.

A woman across the way in the big Lexington House, who seemed to be bedridden for weeks, had a steady stream of stylish, chummy visitors all day long. She lay now in a lazy half-gown through which even I could see the white globes of breasts falling apart to each side and the rosy healthy pantless tummy, the chalky legs slightly apart on the bed, another hopeful crotch seeking the little whiff of air. Still the visitors came, chicly but scantily clad themselves—women in halters, men with rich summer shirts open to the waist. No one bothered or looked, all happily shameless and indifferent to exposure—sexless in the heat. I dreamed about this pleasant middle-aged woman who

had more friends in a week than most of us accumulate in a life-
time. Everybody always laughed in her boudoir, brought her flowers, sipped colored, cool drinks in tall glasses with ice cubes, opened
gift boxes of lingerie on her bed, added to her stacks of books and
magazines by the window sill, and petted her as she laughed them
off with a jolly wave and a greeting to the next group passing them
in the door. Everybody knew everybody and the merry chatter in
the room was palpable. I lay on my stomach in my undies with my
chin in my hands and gaped at the commotion there. For the moment of my gape, I knew that this newly godless postwar atom bomb
city couldn't be utterly lost if one fortyish, fattening, cheerful invalid
could be the convergence of so much love.

In the living room next to her apartment, the thickening, fortyish
man, who *always* seemed to be alone, sat shirtless in the window. His
paper lay on a table; the gray bush on his chest held sweat drops on
the groove between his breasts and stomach. The boxers were spread
at the slit and I could just see a spot of dark soft flesh in the opening
as though his hand had thought to haul it out to cool in the little
whiff and had stopped short, afraid of what it might do there. The
hand lay near on his thigh, his head back against the high chair, eyes
closed, mouth fallen ajar—sleep-dead to lust.

I turned over on my back, my breasts flattened in the stretch
and waited for my turn at the whiff making its rounds of our back-
building world. Summer cauterized the shame and the sex out of
us—leaving us asking for only a brief sigh of air.

The concrete pad with the tree of heaven scaling up between
the building backs to the blasted quadrant of beige sky between
roofs was my community for the summer. Oh, there was the forced
classroom community studying Russian history, a community-space
of isolated integers. Students of summer are aloof. We mulled over
the Boyars, the surfs, and the czars in sweaty solitary under creaking
ceiling fans whose slow revolutions tolled the desultory minutes. As
the Trans-Siberian railroad inched its way across the mummified,
iced-over, wind-massacred Russian arc of the globe—Novgorod, Ir-
kutsk, Novosibirsk—my bottom stayed plastered to the chair with a

glue of sweat. The room lay stagnant, immobile in dank air—a room of dripping faces, sopping shirt backs, and reeking armpits. We were bodies squirming away from the touch of each other. My arm stuck to the page as I took notes about the Russian winter that defeated conqueror after conqueror—but not the New York summer of '53 that silently burned away community, desire, touch—that left you breathless and unable to think of or even *wait* for a better day. In summer you just moved with blank mind and rancid heart through haze trying not to feel your way. I talked to no one in that class. Nobody talked. I scribbled my notes across the watery page and wanted nothing.

And feared nothing. Too hard to fear—loneliness, lovelessness, realities—all chimeras out there on the edge of the sand, mirages that it was too hot to believe in. So I eased my way across the empty desert of New York summer. It stretched before me without oasis or minaret in the distance—goalless—all distractions blasted away. It was if I had awakened from a dream of fearful specters and feverish carryings-on to find myself in this silent, torrid expanse with nothing to do but move with its hot sighs of air. I ate hamburgers in coffee shops on University Place, I ate cheese sandwiches in a Waldorf cafeteria up Lexington, and sat alone for an hour draining a glass of Coke—the *surrruuuppp* of the straw embedded in ice the only sound in a mostly vacant afternoon room. Ceiling fans twirled lazily above, a rhythmic menace tolling in the air like the slow hours before a death that will be weightless. The subways rolled metallically into the oven-stations, and I sat in a void under more revolving fans. It was the strangest state of mind I had ever been in—without desire, with only the barest of needs, sealed in a womb of solitude, safe there, immune to menace.

Moment: one afternoon after class, I sat alone at a basement bar Naomi and I frequented during the year. I drank my Rheingold and a nice young fellow began chatting. There were two of them, and I vaguely recognized them—not as friends or even acquaintances—only as fellow students at Washington Square College. We didn't really talk to each other, just threw out comments into the air above the bar:

"God, nothing to do but drown in beer on an afternoon like this."

"These damn classrooms are murder."

"Even the coldest Russian winter can't penetrate this New York summer."

"Imagine a chem lab—heat on heat until you vaporize into extinction."

They were science guys. The one next to me, with his open shirt, brush cut, and clear-skinned boyish look was genial and captivating for the moment. He stood tall above the bar and talked lightly without intention or motive. I finished my beer. His friend asked my name and said, "I'm Dan ___ and this," putting a hand on the genial one's shoulder—both of them grinning for no reason, "this is John ___." "Okay," I got up. "Well, Liz, keep cool—a joke, of course, and have a nice weekend." "You too. So long," and I left.

On Monday morning, *The Daily News* ran a story about a student named John at Washington Square College of NYU, who over the weekend had murdered his mother in their apartment on Park Avenue. He had stabbed her and then called the police to come for him. A quote from the paper: "I would come to the station myself, but one more blast of heat would finish me. We are air-conditioned here. So I'll be waiting."

"Amazing," I thought. "How very nice he was," and felt no terror in the aftermath. In the desert, all things are mirages, even the waters of salvation and hellfire itself.

Moment: After a couple of weeks of silence, the phone rang one afternoon. It was Lenny Marcus, the mordant older vet, sidekick to pal Manny, whom I had been in subterranean love with since sophomore year. He had known, of course, as I had sulked and mooned around him off and on for months. He was quiet and had a wide thin mouth that stretched across his face in a line that I found tragic and irresistible. His grin made you want to cry. He chuckled at Manny and at private jokes and went to racetracks and departing ocean liners on the Hudson piers: "Want to go to a party, Liz? Just pick a ship that's leaving, go up the gang plank on board and there are a hundred parties going on—just take your pick—all the booze you can drink until they blow the horn and you stagger off covered with confetti and wrapped in ribbons and kissed by every beautiful dame in first class! They're the greatest parties in New York." And so we did—carousing from cabin to cabin, deck to deck, lovable strangers being hugged and kissed and champagned to death—and then off, waving and screaming to our unknown voyagers and hosts—and then to part at our subways with a "So long, see ya, kid," and no kiss. I found him tenderly cynical and irresistible. For a year, he found me cute, serious, young, and scary. I peeled off in my junior year, probably disappointed and glad to grow up on Bill Glass and his martinis. Lenny had moved to the back room of my heart that had given up on love for the season.

Until that telephone rang: "Hi, Liz, Lenny Marcus." "My gosh, Lenny, really! I'm surprised. How are you?" He had never called me before. I didn't conceive that he would know my number. There had never been the remotest chance of giving it to him. He had carefully kept our contact to cafeteria dates. "Manny gave me your number. God, it's hot. Much too hot to go to the racetrack. So what are you doing? Haven't seen you around much this year."

"Nothing much," I answered. "Summer school course . . ."

Silence.

"Say, are you alone?"

"Yeah, I'm living alone here, going to finish college this fall. My mother moved to Connecticut."

Silence.

"Are you busy? How about I come up there for a while?"

"Okay, I'm here."

So he came up, knocked, I let him in, we delivered stray phrases to each other for ten minutes, he sat beside me on my mother's old cot of fornication, kissed me, fondled my braless breast, pulled up the skirt, lay me down, said, "Do you have a diaphragm?" I shook my head. He sighed, "Okay, not the best, but guess I have to," took out a rubber and unrolled it down and came inside, pushed up a few times, caught his breath above me and shrunk out. Kissed me on the cheek. "Okay, sorry, Liz, that's it," chagrin on the wide mouth, distance and pathos in the faint blue eyes. "Guess it's not always what it's cracked up to be. Guess I'll be going." He held my hand at the door. "Sorry. Good luck. See ya around in the cafeteria in the fall. I'll be taking courses for the duration."

The first man I had slept with in four years. Yes, I had kept my vow not to sleep with a man until I loved him—until my heart truly yearned. Lenny had come to me in the desert of summer and had killed my love cleanly as if by plan, as if doing me a favor. It had worked. The last suppressed desire of my heart had died along with everything else in the whiff of air now trailing in from the tree of heaven that blessed us all in the back building world of 681.

Moment: I remember a weekend afternoon in Saybrook. I am sitting in an alien world of blue sky and cool winds softening over the marshes that stretch away behind my mother's backyard. I am not at home, but I am happy for a weekend of surcease from the oppressive beige vapor that lies stagnant over Lexington Avenue. We are lounging on chairs under Mom's majestic elm tree that waves in stately glory even as it's dying, as are most of the elms along Main Street. Up high, whole arching branches are shriveling. At least for now I don't regret the tree of heaven that had probably a generation ago broken through the trash-ridden concrete earth of Manhattan and risen up five stories, immune to exotic infestation, nourished and gladdened by its grime. We few visitors from the grime sit in exile under the lazy, swaying branches of this ancient fragile monarch, talking of the world.

"Of course, they will step on Poland. They always have, my Russians. You will see." Marya, Alan Harrington's girlfriend, is speaking of world events—Iron Curtain disturbances and the endlessly intriguing specter of Russia. Marya and Alan are up for the weekend to visit John and Shirley. Alan is contorting his long torso around a lawn chair, amused by his own enigmatic comments that murmur through his feminine lips. His cheeks are hollowed and boned like those of a thin, stunning woman. "Of course, my dear, you speak from an ever so slightly outdated affinity." "Oh, shut up, Harrington. You couldn't know. Russia is always the same—whether czarist or Soviet, the names make no difference." Marya talks with an affable growl and is unfazed by Alan, unimpressed by his wit, bored by his Harvard education, belittling of his towering height above her.

I have described her in one of my novels, *Cass Wiley Leaves*. She's some sort of Russian, ex-ballet dancer from St. Petersburg by way of Paris, now dumpy with only the oddly tight calf muscles left from her dancing days—unnaturally poised as though always on point, where the rest of her has gone naturally to fat. Her round stomach sticks out like a beach ball over which she wears splotchy red tops. Black darting little pig's eyes, archy black eyebrows, and black tightly waved hair parted in the middle and fanning out to her shoulders, making a pyramid of her head. Pasty white face and thick flat lips painted a scarlet that is renewed all day. Now she pulls the floppy, grieving ears of her little basset hound who sprawls across her lap. She is impatient with intellectual chatter and refuses to acknowledge veiled repartee, which John and Alan often get off on. She swears and is slangy and dismissive of literary puffery and subtlety. "You think you know Russia—you literary boys panting at the feet of your goddamn beloved Dostoyevsky! All those books infested with runty little Nihilist vermin running around ratty garrets. You think—ah, the Russian soul!" John and Alan shut up and smile with habitual tolerance, but they listen. Marya flounces and dismisses with rotund authority. Shirley giggles, my mother pours some tea, and we all wait because somehow Marya knows things we all don't. Here is Alan's new woman, and she skirts all the usual prophecies and revelations and intellectual pronouncements I'm used to. Now, at twenty and having been through a minor mill myself, she opens my door.

"Tell us, Marya, tell us the secret of the Russian soul."

"Aaach! It's a lazy, dreaming, gloomy sort of thing. Stupid, really—not deep and dark and world-shaking like you boys like to think. Listen! You want the Russian soul? Close your *Karamazovs* and *Idiots*—read *Oblomov*, read Goncharov! That is the essence of Russia. Lying around in its dirty dressing gown—and occasionally rising up in a reckless binge of loving and bullying. Hah! That's the *real* Russia!"

I know I hadn't read Goncharov. I don't know whether John and Alan had. They laugh knowingly enough, but they don't say anything. Marya guffaws triumphantly at them. "There's your precious Russian soul. Lazy and suffering. Yes, suffering only from its dreams!"

Yes, my door stays open under Marya's carefree assault on John and Alan's intellectual hegemony. It's clear they don't lay down any laws for her—and for the first time John's often ruthless authority over my timid mind evaporates under the dying elm and the cool laughing Russian air of a Connecticut summer. Oh, I warmed to this Marya from old Petersburg. "Can I buy this *Oblomov*? Is it available? I'm taking Russian history this summer, and this will clarify the picture. See . . ." (I can't stop.) "I've already learned this Soviet thing's just a continuation of old Russian patterns—the exile system goes way back—the brutality of purges, Ivan the Terrible. Even the cultured Western ones— Peter, Catherine with the wild savage streak. So I've got to read *Oblomov*!"

"I have it. Come see me in Queens and I'll give it to you," Marya turns to me and growls out this invitation, ignoring the "boys" as she calls them, and patting my knee. This unusually long speech from me must have awakened her. She appears to make an instant decision to cultivate me for her own curious, self-interested reasons. She is not vague. "Come next Wednesday—if you're free—at three o'clock, and we will walk Mischa together and have tea in a glass, Russian style after. Okay?" I agree at once. I am free most afternoons, after all, if for basement beers with matricides and love-killing coitus on my mother's old cot, then certainly for this scornful, dumpy Russian woman who seems to have acquired such a distinct purpose for me.

Perhaps I am just bristling under old authority and respond instantly to her egalitarian recklessness. Here is this spirited, heavy-featured, faded Harrington mistress who tears the ancient idols off their pedestals and brings them down with mortal men without a thought. I sense dimly that this aging dancer might just be a fresh branch of the old tree of knowledge I have left behind this year to frolic and flounder in the shadows of the tree of life—all this drinking and hangover and loveless sex and summer ennui. Well, Marya stirs freshening breezes and, with a gruff appointment, wrenches my summer into direction.

We went back to the city on different trains, and starting that Wednesday I went to see Marya three times a week for the rest of the summer. I don't recall another weekend in Saybrook or any more solitary beers and bedmates. Marya and her little Mischa (if that was his name), her raucous, violent diatribes, and her occult uses for me were enough. In the mornings, I sat under the tired ceiling fan of the classroom and nailed down the bones of Russian history, building up my own Slavic skeleton in a paper on Catherine the Great. Then in the afternoons I got drunk on a torrent of Russian love and hate—a Volga of excitability that never ran dry—until it was truly for me the Russian summer of '53 in Queens, New York.

Marya lived in an apartment complex in some place like Astoria, a place I'd never been. I took unfamiliar IND trains out of Manhattan to emerge in sunny open squares with trees, more sky, shopping centers, and no buildings over ten stories, an un-downtown part of New York that was as strange to me as Indianapolis or Kiev would be. I made my way up an elevator in one of the buildings in the complex to Marya's floor, walked down a carpeted hall to her door, rang the discreet bell with its two-note jingle—a type of entrance unheard of in my Manhattan, and enter Marya, center stage.

"I'm coming, right there, Liz—aaaach, Mischa, you'll trip me, you little monster baggage of death—I swear, Liz, he will kill me on the way to the door—aaach, I must live through another day with this mutt . . . Oh, oh, oh, gorgeous little Mischa—it's all right, darling, mother adores you. Aaach, not another day . . . , " she opens the door, "Aah, Liz. Come in, come in, a beautiful afternoon for our walk with the little monster. Aaach, not another day with that rat, Harrington!"

And the afternoon begins. "Ah, ah, sit down, have a glass of cold tea and a *syrniki* with cherry jam—there is the most magnificent Russian bakery on Queen's Plaza—we'll go sometime—while I tell you the latest from that six-foot-four gangly nincompoop. Supposed to come last night for dinner at six. Shows up half-potted on some cocktail bash about eight and my blinis are stale and the cold borscht is sitting warm on the table and the *pelmeny* are cold on the stove and all he wants to do is drink vodka and tonics anyway and blubber on about loving me and not being able to put up with everything—hah, all those fancy drinks and pretty young blondes—'nubile' he calls them. Huff—a regular Humbert Humbert he is. You know that, Liz. Anyway, all this horse dung he throws around my living room—to hell with my perfect Russian dinner I have slaved over—just more vodka—and then—the giant moron—all he wants is a tussle in the sheets, in which, by the way, he can't perform and passes out! And he calls us 'besotted Russians'! That's his word, 'besotted'! I tell you, Liz—isn't that cheese fritter *the* most sublime? I'm breaking up with Harrington tonight! It's over!"

She wears tight beige Bermuda shorts that expose a couple of inches of lumpy thighs above still slim knees and those eternally taut calves. Hooked and gnarled toes with scarlet tips stick out of white high platform sandals—a concession to those calves with their old longing to lift. She fusses inside the shoulder of the magenta top for a stray bra strap. She hauls it up until a white strip shows neck-side. Six inches of flamboyant bracelets ring out with every movement of heavily bejeweled hands and these are dancing all over—scrabbling in her purse for keys, feeling on tabletops and sofabacks for Mischa's leash, pulling on his forlorn ears, patting her hair, repainting her lips, finally guiding Mischa and me to the door, "Let's go quickly, quickly, before that limp sad sack calls to check up on me." This calls for a complicitous smile from me, which calls for, "Yes, imagine—that complaining molester of young girls is jealous! Calls me six times a day with 'Where are you going this afternoon? Where were you this morning—coffee-ing with that faded ridiculous exiled Russian doctor on the third floor?'"

She's locking the door with a jangle of wrist armor, then bends all the way down, her ample beige butt upended, to smooch the nose of Mischa, who wriggles in happy hysteria. "Kiss that little nose, Liz—and put an ice cube to your lips! Ah, he's the best little lover a poor old, fat Russian lady's got!" I do as I am told, as life yaws helplessly before Marya's Russian gale.

We hit the street and perambulate around the open square and through small green spaces. Mischa pulls and tugs at the leash and stops at every protuberance from the ground. Marya indulges him with a running commentary on each. "Fancy new red hydrant just for you, darling! Oh, not on the trash basket with all the dirty papers—no, no, not dainty at all. Now, there, gorgeous, is a beautiful bush. You can sneak way under and do your big business while Liz and I keep watch. Isn't he the most elegant little ballerina this side of Petersburg!"

We dip in and out of shops on the square. Out of her purse that dangles among the bracelets on her arm she takes an expandable string bag which she begins to fill with one or two items from each store—two Vidalia onions here, a bunch of fresh beets at a market, potato *vareniky* at a deli, black bread and blinis at the bakery, a small tin of red caviar at a specialty shop. "Will you tell me, Liz, why do I do it? This Caspian Sea delicacy for that schlunk with his shirttails hanging out? Why? Why?"

When the bag is full we head back across the plaza. The late af-ternoon sun is tired and drops its moist light on the wilted streets. Mischa's ears flop to the sidewalk and his tiny bandy legs puddle along slowly beside the platform sandals; his mouth hangs open, and his eyes droop ahead with his valiant doggy effort to keep up with Mama. And Mama up there keeping up with him, a patina of moisture highlight-ing the fine hairs of her cheeks near the ears. I trudge along beside the couple, carrying the string bag, submerged in facial sweat and trying to escape my armpits and inner thighs. Heat fatigue spreads us out across the sidewalk. Marya's engine is running down, so that when she meets the doctor from the third floor—who is small and gray with a Stalin-mustache and tiny scared eyes behind round rimless glasses— she pats his arm, kisses her lips, and presses the fiery fingertips against the bushy mouth. "Ah, Doctor Igor, not a day to be out in that hot gray suit like armor. You will melt away inside! Too hot for real kisses. Oh, by the way, I got some marvelous *syrniki* and raspberry jam at the Shulov Bakery. Full of seeds and ripe sour sting. Come and enjoy them with me for morning coffee. *Da svedanya*, little man." Mischa wags a cordial tail up at the little doctor, who walks in pathos.

We enter the cool, carpeted apartment with its chintz-flowered sofa, chairs, tea table, and the filtered sun coming through the glass curtains. There are very good drawings and lithographs on the walls—a Malevich non-objective and even a tiny Chagall. She has pointed them out to me with no particular pride, as though they

come with the genes and her full and complicated history of exile, which she has never dwelled on. She is just matter-of-factly a
woman of depth (with her translations of underground compatriot
poets), and by late afternoon she is meditative and her tone becomes
weary and philosophical. She casts remote insights over our current
lives and those who people them.

I am mildly surprised each afternoon, when the tirades wind
down to these musing codas, at how much thought she gives to me.
"Yes, Liz, of course, you are very much in awe of your big brother. I
can imagine he is a kind of god to you with his books and articles.
But he is really just a nice, serious boy—a good, thoughtful boy who
is caught between two lives. He's human like the rest of us." I nod
my head and am silent, which leads her into further exegesis.

"You probably liked Marian, eh?"

"Yes, I did—like my real sister."

"Well, you've got to move on now. It's probably a good thing
they broke up—for *you*, I mean. I'll bet it took him off his pedestal
for you. Good for you to see him floundering a little and moving on
to a new girl. We're all a bunch of old gray carps bumping around
blindly in our tanks." She puts a tall glass of cold tea and another
small cheese fritter in front of me, and I wait for her to plow further
in this field that runs close to my current confusion.

"I'll bet he talked your head off."

"Yes, yes, he did all through my high school years. Introduced
me to everything—poetry, books, bebop . . ." ("Ugh!" she broke in.)
"crazy people and parties and Beatness . . . and *Russia*."

"Russia! Oh, my God! I know, I know—he and Alan intellec-
tualizing the heart of the world away. All they do is *talk*! Though
Johnny's a nice boy, considerate. Sometimes I wonder how he puts
up with Harrington. I confess, he seems intimidated as though Alan
is some intellectual wizard casting spells over lesser minds. Oh, Liz,
were you that way with John? Yes, I see it!"

I don't have to answer. She now becomes the icon-breaker and
begins to work up some twilight fury in the cool, quiet living room.
Her rings flash and her cigarette holder waves about. "Aaaah, that's
no good, Liz. Like my stupid Russians lugging heavy morbid icons

through their lives—they used to be down-in-the-mouth saints on rusty tin. Now it's Lenin and Stalin posters. It makes no difference—all icons to cringe before and enforce dressing-gown laziness. You are thinking for *yourself* now and getting out of John's intellectual dressing gown. I'm here to tell you, it's good, Liz!" Then, "Aaaah!" She brushes the crumbs off her fingers passionately. "Harrington, an icon! He's a disorderly slob, selfish up to his armpits, arrogant over his 'brilliant' wit and 'astute' insights—which are only overripe, rotting intellectual footnotes gleaned from Harvard lecture halls and musty libraries that don't live a minute when they hit the air of real life. Look at how he treated that silly, poor Virginia—stuffing her in that rat's nest and running off to get drunk in the filthy Chelsea asylum of that debauched old classmate, the daemonic roach of Manhattan that they all prated about and worshipped as their very own Satan! Oh, you know . . . what was his name—Italian sounding?"

"Cannastra, Bill Cannastra, Marya."

"Yes, see, you know all about it—got it firsthand from John. Oh, but really—it's all playacting. There's not a really crazy bone in Harrington's whole lanky frame! He's an imposter, Liz. After his little games, his trifles and flirtations with blond twenty-year-olds, he comes home to dumpy old *real* Russian mamooshka, Marya. And with that front tail of his, dangling no good between his legs. Well, he bullied that poor sweet, stupid Virginia. Oh, I know, you probably liked her too, but I'm sorry, we both must see things as they are. Goddamn it, I've been fighting Russian sentimentality—all that pitiful Slavic bathos—for decades. Oh well, I'm furious most of the time with this great writer/lover of mine! He sits and complains night after night—his writing isn't appreciated, his books aren't recognized or read, he has to do hackwork to live, he never sees his son who really bores him anyway. 'How can you have an intelligent discussion with a three-year-old!' he says, slumped in self-pity, bitching and complaining to the air while I pour black coffee into him. But I tell him to go to hell as I pour. How have I stood him a whole year now? And he even wanted to move in here, but he really wanted me to move into his beloved Manhattan and pay outrageous rent so he

can live on upper Madison Avenue. Oh, oh, oh! It's over now, this
minute! The endless quarreling has killed it. I'll tell him it's finished
tonight! Oh, oh, oh!"

She clicks briskly now on her high platforms in and out of the
kitchen, working herself up to a fiery cold lather of frustration.
About this time I am in awe and sorrow, for she is so genuinely and
absurdly mad at herself, in a rage at her own full, strong heart. I am
so sorry, for at this precise moment three times a week, when the
sun fades and she brings the vodka and tonic out for a drink before I
leave, I love her so much for making me so clear and herself so mired
in paradox. For I know what will happen right now at five o'clock.

The phone rings. "Yes, dear, what's the matter? . . . Can't Peggy take
it to Harcourt? . . . Oh, well, it's too bad, of course, but tell them to
shove it . . . Well, no . . . I'm busy with translations . . . Oh, shit . . . I'm
sure you cried plenty on Peggy's sexy shoulder . . . Oh, yes, I know,
I'm still the best sack mate you've got . . . Shut up, Harrington! Don't
blubber so. It sickens me . . . Well, yes, babooshka, you're sweet . . . Okay
. . . come along then. But no gloomy faces, promise? . . . Yes, we'll go
out to dinner. I'm not cooking tonight in all this heat—and all you do
is drink here anyway . . . Oh, I've got some sublime red caviar . . . So
yes, darling, come for vodka and red heaven . . . So long, dear."

She hangs up and I get up to leave. "Well, Liz, you see how it
goes. Anyway, icons are for worship, worship isn't love. Love is for
the rest of us. What can I do? Love is for slobs like Harrington." I'm
at the door, she holds Mischa in her arms for me to kiss his cold
nose. Then we kiss cheeks. "It will end someday—maybe soon—but
not tonight, I guess. Come Friday for little Mischa and me, and I'll
fix you wonderful blinis with honey."

So I would come Friday and the next Monday, Wednesday, and
Friday after class to Queens and then further across this Russian
steppe with its confounding landscape of advance and retreat, love
and scorn, honey and sour cherry jam. Marya was delightful and
made a lark of my summer. Anger and disdain from her lips fresh-
ened the dead, rank city breezes. The East River was a Lethe that
I crossed three times a week to forget the ninety-degree cloud of

exhaust and angst that entombed Lexington Avenue, killing all hope
and despair. My heart came alive in Queens, listening to each fresh
tale of frustration. Marya's litany of harmony-in-discord was a mel-
ody I could count on, but with odd tender off-notes, "But he's really
a sweet boy under the arrogant claptrap. He drools over my Chicken
Kiev." Learning her tune was a new way of knowledge—Marya's
lessons of the human heart from the Russian angle. While sopping
up her sweet cheese fritters, I learned the pith of her lesson—simply
the true reality of love—how its *modus operandi* is paradox, how it
rarely rests, and feeds on a certain amount of storm and battle. And
that its survival is always open to question. I also learned that all men
are mortal—even Harrington, even brother John.

After Labor Day, busy lives took up again. I started my full fall
schedule. And Marya? I don't remember seeing her after a late summer afternoon when she had played her balalaika tune of Har-
rington-crimes and Marya-lively sufferings a final time, "Good luck
your last semester. Call if you need anything. I'm here—at least
for now. The big slob is nagging like hell to get me to Manhattan.
But *enough!* Good-bye, little Liz. Don't forget little Mischa." I bend
down to kiss them both—Mischa of the weeping ears and eyes and
the little dumpy woman for whom all beings large and small walk
in pathos and need her cross and spacious heart. I remember my
Melville. Ah, Russia, ah humanity.

Chapter 11

End of College—Beat and Bop Leftovers

—— Labor Day—fall—signal of beginnings, opening of a new season, the air cooling with pungent promise—always in my mind, John and Jack's declaring the start of a season of parties, and the bars and apartments jammed with overwrought people flush with excitement, astounding words pouring out, delicious acrid smoke in the air and the latest tenor sax—who this season? Why, man, don'tcha know, Trane gyrating on from Bird, solemn young killer sax man blowing everywhere—September, October, New York, new sounds, new revelers in the streets, new gone weed in from Mexico or Louisiana, new lovers, new visions. Jesus, man, new life!

September 1953, 681. Fall opened in businesslike fashion with the routine litany of classes—Modern American Literature, Modern Poetry, British History II, Film Literature, and who knows the last—another history course, economics, required speech put off until the end. It hardly mattered. I'd read modern American literature and modern poetry. From high school on, it had burrowed into the marrow of my bones. Nothing here bore the air of discovery. So I listened to Eda Lou Walton, a wilting Greenwich Village rose, gossip about Hart Crane throwing boomerangs at parties on Horatio Street, and the saga of his women stealing Lawrence's ashes back and forth across the ocean and continent until nobody really knows what's in that urn in Taos, New Mexico. I plodded yet again through Hemingway, Fitzgerald, and Faulkner and tried to find something new for myself by writing a paper on Robert Penn Warren. My fellow classmates and I watched the renowned Latin American scholar, Henry Bamford Parkes, nod off to sleep, head tilted, eyelids dropping as he sat on the desk lecturing. We then turned aside in stale embarrassment as Professor Gessner spent a whole semester dissecting the screenplay of John Huston's *The Red Badge of Courage*, a story I had read in high school, and with a tired hand on his crotch, leering lazily at the girls. Last semester in college—postmortem effects.

John was living mostly in Saybrook where he and Shirley were beginning a major, backbreaking overhaul of the house behind my mother's—tearing down walls for a huge living room, kitchen, and dining room decorated with John's darkly varnished copies of ship paintings, and book and record cases lining the walls. Out of an old school building that was a warren of cubicles, they created a darkened, time-encrusted stately eccentric lady of a country villa. John and Shirley renovated and fermented a domicile like the aging of the rich burnish of a consummate bourbon—and whispered to me one weekend that they had gotten married and no one must know— and they would emerge from the wood a perfected fact like the two miraculous bugs from Melville's "Apple Tree Table." But from New York? Gone. Just a few pieces of furniture and some dusty herbs in the kitchen of Shirley's pad at 123 Lexington. Jack gone, Ginsberg gone, the Beat orbit shifting away across the continent to San Francisco, Alan in partial exile in Queens with Marya, Virginia recovering in Connecticut, my mother also in Connecticut going serenely to seed at her kitchen table.

But in my new businesslike, morning approach to life I had passed through grieving over abandonment. The long and suffering wake of last spring and summer had ended, and the days of revelation were put to the ground in decent burial, but with eyes turned away and feet trodding the last lap toward completion—with relief, without exhilaration. A ho-hum season, this fall. I looked for little more than the mild familiar pleasures of leftovers. They would do for a time—and after all, the time would be short. Sometime in the early months of the new year, I would be the last unsung and youngest member of a short, seven-year generation that passed through and forged at least a small revolution of life and spirit at 681 Lexington Avenue.

It was a strange fall season for me, precisely as it was the dullest. I wrote A papers out of mental stagnation, although I did work up some heat over that Robert Penn Warren essay. The professor—who was head of the English department—applauded it and offered to write glowing letters for me to graduate schools. It seems that I had made a turn toward teaching. I was relieved but not ecstatic. In the great scheme of things it was a bit of an anticlimax to descend from a fever over Faulkner (A year ago I had spent a whole summer devouring his books.) to reading grand themes into Robert Penn Warren. My professor was probably telling me with his applause that I would some day, quite competently, narrow myself down for the PhD. Oh, oh, oh, this was not a season of grand themes.

My professors' eccentricities were amusing—not exciting. Oh, there were moments. I remember standing in the back of a large class-room among scores of auditors, listening to a tall gray-haired man with a small, compact paunch and a cigarette holder, who slouched against the desk and talked out softly to the ambient air of existentialism. The most popular course that year in philosophy: Existentialism, Professor William Barrett—a man who many of us had seen off-hours at the Minetta Tavern or San Remo's. I don't remember his words. After all, I had gotten his living, breathing message from John years before. Professor Barrett made a living out of existentialism. It was the mental furniture of his brain and, in postwar fifties New York, it was profitable. It fit him like the tired gray suit he slouched in. John's gang had plunged into the living of it, risking all and refusing its depressing connotations. No, they dashed around in the throes of it searching for a new brand of exaltation. So I stood with the crowds, left only with the frisson of solidarity and publicity. Professor Barrett was our popularizer of existentialism with his books and his articles in *The New York Times*. After all, we all knew we were existential now.

There was one electric college moment, though. Naomi persuaded me to go to an English department reading. She had become something of a student leader in the English Club and had already gotten into the English Honors Society. A couple of Bs had kept me out, and I was already too jaded for English Club luncheon soirées. She had told me enough—a languid T.S. Eliot sipping tea with an extended finger. He was all the rage in those days, but I had been schooled on Blake and Yeats and Lawrence and called him "Tough Shit" Eliot. I never joined the English Club, already sniffing out stuffiness in the ranks of college literature.

But Naomi said Dylan Thomas was reading this afternoon and, of course, "You can't call *him* stuffy!" I went and sat in the last row of a long narrow room reserved for these talks. Of course, we all knew how he roared around New York, leaving a wake of alcoholic outrage and riot behind—the roly-poly man with the spitting mouth and booming voice, goosing and scandalizing Manhattan literati. We all knew the stories—the raging wife who would come to drag him away, *The Partisan Review*-niks hovering ever near to scoop up the last words. Many of us had witnessed his act at the White Horse Tavern on Hudson and hung around the Chelsea Hotel to catch a glimpse of his hungover disorder.

Well, Thomas swayed up at the podium, far off from me with my telescopic view. The voice came from far away, deeply resonating, strong, as though the distance only augmented it. In the front rows, it might have erupted like a muddy growl of static. But through the dark, long air of the room, the bass voice purified and the words came clear like the hollow voice of God booming out from the deepest cavern with words you dare not mistake. Stirring and dangerous that voice was. It rumbled through my entrails. He didn't talk. He read his and others' poems. I heard the words and knew the poems. John had read many of them years before in my living room under the skylight. The message now was in the medium—the voice. He was clearly drunk and mindless of this collegiate gathering. He lurched and grabbed the podium with both hands. Even in the back I could hear the spit come out with the s's.

Finally, he announced the last poem with no introduction. "Last I'll read 'Lapis Lazuli' by W.B.Yeats." It boomed down lower and lower through "the fiddle-bow," "Hamlet and Lear," "camel-back, horseback ... Old civilizations put to the sword ..." lower, deeper, building melancholy until I felt the world crack open and this cosmic thunder explode out to rend us all. Then—pause—the decibel lowered, the tone shifted, and I saw far up on the mountain "Two Chinamen, behind them a third / Are carved in lapis lazuli," like a sly whisper from the "cherry branch" up there, and fingers, like the breath of the clearest mountain air, begin to play the coda, which I knew so well. The living poet's voice lightened like a spring breeze from the river. Where was he going, even though I knew? How was he going to get there? There was no way to tell with this new, high singsong voice. "Their eyes"—up, breaking off, "mid many wrinkles," resting on the plateau, "their ancient glittering eyes ... " stop, the air now so high, so thin—on Chinese Everest we are ". . . gay"—the word tilting up, up into the silence. I must be shivering now, I am breathless up here with that word. These were not the lines I had heard John bearing down in doom at 681. No, these were God's final benedictions to us. God quoting Yeats. Poor God—humbled to the wisdom and words of his creature. Great God—his vision manifested in the dead poet's words and transmitted in the voice of the live one.

Thomas stumbled off the platform, a professorial arm steadying him. I never saw him again, never went to another reading—never cared to. The ineffable tilt up of Yeats' last word to us, "gay ..." almost with a question mark, is the final, mystical note of my literary consciousness. Thomas died that November of 1953.

★ ★ ★ ★

We were all in a bit of a flurry over films that fall. It was the time of cinemascope and that bland, bullying declaration flashing over Times Square—"Movies Are Better Than Ever!" We gushed over *Asphalt Jungle*, *All About Eve*, *A Place in the Sun*, and ranted against *Duel In the Sun*. We argued over obscure Harold Lloyd shorts and

Griffith's *Intolerance*, rating it high above *Birth of a Nation*, which by the way, we never scorned for its racism, and we were all left-ies. As film buffs, we didn't consider racism a relevant category. We talked in terms of zoom shots, angles, cutting and splicing, and went around making boxes of our fingers in everybody's face. I shouldn't say "we," because film stuff was mostly a diversion for me, and these guys, Charlie Baum, Malcolm Weiner, and the others were smart, lighthearted, and technical. It was a happy time, being in on the ground floor of an art form. The great, unwashed mob saw movies as wonderful dream-stuff; my film pals found bits and pieces of art in the worst of them. They haunted the ancient silent film series at the Museum of Modern Art (I had seen even Charlie Chaplin's five-minute shorts.) and the Thalia uptown for foreign films, just now beginning to astound the little crowd of initiates.

Bob Gessner was the founder and chairman of the NYU film department, and he was a locally renowned lecher. He's gone now, but I don't think he would mind the designation. After all, he made history in his way. His little department of two—himself and the tire-less, maniacal craftsman Haig Manoogian—had the only film cache outside of Southern California. It swelled up in Gessner's wake and produced film geniuses like Martin Scorsese and Spike Lee. Gessner had the vision, and, once setting it in motion, like God, he rested. The funky, eager little film buffs—many of them my pals—who took all the courses for the first degrees in cinema, had a romp pil-laring and defaming him. Oh, the cafeteria talk—ribald, nasty, good-humored. Item: He leched after all the girls, he drooled, he lazed and didn't give a fart for the courses, he made a slave out of the humble, faithful Haig, and his eyelids drooped lewdly over blue eyes that stayed fixated on the legs and breasts in front of him. He sat with his hard corpulent gut exposed by the open jacket, a pipe in his mouth and a hand fingering his crotch. He sat aslant the desk for all to see while he droned on over the *Red Badge* screenplay.

So naturally all the film buffs scorned and trampled on the lewd, languid Dr. Gessner, their very own father who was unforgivably bored by the baby he'd created. How dare he not give a fuck—yawn and play with himself over the sacred new art? Well, he did. He'd written his books, inaugurated the first East Coast film school, and, what the hell, wasn't that enough? I look back on him now and say that he'd had his gravity and broken new ground and converted a new generation (Haig was clearly a grateful slave.). So give a man his vision and let him go. Besides, the little gang loved him, held him close in their hearts, where they handled him with care—their very own fallen idol—even as they trashed him. Besides again, in all of it, the corpulent tummy, the hand working on his fly, the mouth foaming about the pipe, the randy leer—in all the fleshy excess of him there was a salacious charm.

Deep in our hearts—or in the Venus mound between our legs—we few girls in the group fell for him every time. Okay, to use that mangled, misused contemporary word that covers more crimes than blessings, it was liberating to know exactly what the old fatso was after when he made his moves and, for that very reason, not know how far he'd get with them. When the plays of the game were laid out bald and bold like he did, there could only be surprise to jazz it up. It was fun to wonder how far you'd go—when would you turn it off—would you turn it off—how would he respond to the advances and retreats? The result was that quite a few girls went at least a few steps into the Gessner game.

He took me for coffee one morning at a dreary shop nearby that most students avoided for unknown reasons. It was too dark, not enough tables for a proper gang, or the manager wasn't student-friendly. Who knows why groups settle into some hangouts and avoid others. Anyway, Gessner steered me unerringly to this shunned shop. We spent a bored half hour fingering our cups and not saying much. It was known that he tested all the girls—he was a sensual democrat, equal opportunity for all—but that some failed, though that F was secreted in the dumped girl's heart. He didn't seem too interested in me. His look and talk dropped off when the cup was half gone. I was awed and quiet and serious, always fancying love lurking at the edges of the most flagrant lust. My grave eyes with their melancholy droop amused him, but they couldn't hold him long. He stood up—immense and tweedy above me—smiling down benignly and taking my elbow as I followed suit. "Well, Miss Holmes, this has been delightful. You're certainly an interesting, serious girl. Time for class." The interview was over.

Pass, fail? I couldn't tell for sure, although I feared. He didn't ask for more. I was in a dither. Charlie would be rolling his eyes at me in the cafeteria. They were sure to have watched our stroll down the block. There wasn't much to report. I would keep my fears to myself. But Professor Gessner had gone from being a lecher to a wonder to me and now *I* wanted more. Oh yes, over coffee I had fallen for the charm of lechery. Because it was there around the ho-hum talk, lurking at the edges of his eyes and slumping with his jowls—there in the faint drops of spittle left by the pipe, in the wedding ring on his finger and that hand resting sentiently on his lap. There it all was— supreme lechery—confident in every detail, saying louder than the conversation: "There is *this*, and there is nothing more." Later I was muffled and miserable, certain I was not up to the mark.

He called me a couple of weeks later, not soon, but not too long for the fade-out. Would I like to go to a matinee—*Julius Caesar* with Brando? It was a critical puzzlement, this performance—*enfant terrible* wrenching Shakespeare into the method. Did Dr. Gessner think me an intellectual piece? I supposed so, but was not especially flattered by the thought. The priapic urge would latch on to any method, after all.

So we went to a midtown theater and sat in the mezzanine and watched Brando simulate and stimulate public grief in a Hell's Kitchen[15] voice—Actor's Studio stuff. And he was *good*. The good professor slouched next to me and worked a heavy arm around my shoulders, all the while slurping a chuckle at the wonder boy on the screen. He clearly enjoyed the performance and coughing and growling as he did was as serious a critique as he could give. I think he'd seen the film already anyway—maybe with Jean Nussbaum, a dark beauty in the class, who had all the guys foaming at the mouth. I froze up at the

---

15. Editor's Note: Hell's Kitchen is an area of Manhattan located approximately between Thirty-fourth Street and Fifty-ninth Street, and from Eighth Avenue to the Hudson River. It was once home to impoverished Irish-Americans and mobsters.

thought. I was not in her league. He fondled my shoulder and paid little attention to the rest of the film, all standard British-accent Roman. He took me for something afterwards, I hardly remember what. I guess he kissed me in the scrofulous vestibule to 681. But something stopped him—perhaps the sting of alcoholic urine in his nostrils, the torn-up rubber padding on the stairs, the certainty of roaches lying in wait—God knows—or just the four-flight climb through this derelict precinct. Something tamped down the mildly aroused libido, and he left with a really kindly smile. I failed, but the gentle smile told me that he didn't hold it against me.

Oh well, life went on. I repeated the matinee-tale but smirked away the insinuating questions. I took up with the rumor-trashing of "old Bob" with the others again, mildly mad, and feeling that I would be damned if I would *ever* expose the kindly other face of the libertine. Fuck him (which I had not come close to doing, so easy as it was said to be). But behind the snicker we suppressed in the classroom, I, for one, found him actually endearing with his soft leering eyes and his hand on his fly.

★ ★ ★ ★

Things happened that fall, but nothing struck deep. Of course, I loved bop and still whistled away many solitary hours by the phonograph, repeating old solos and new cool "white" ones from the West Coast that I was buying. Stan Getz and the Brothers—I learned them all and could bandy their names: Brew Moore, Zoot Sims, Alan Eager, Al Cohn, and Bob Brookmeyer—cool with a limpid, fragile jump and pretty codas that vanished into the air. These guys had been around a long time, but they were the jazz vogue now; the world was cooling down. Dizzy was going commercial, Monk was getting weirder, Parker was drowning in strings and otherwise falling apart, and Bud Powell, my own ecstatic Bud, was rotting away in the Creedmore madhouse—like the Rockland Ginsberg was soon to howl about in San Francisco. My boyfriend, Howie, had dropped away into his own musical scene. I never saw him again. I didn't go to Birdland—every

other set was filled with the bloated roar of Wild Bill Davis on organ
and Pee Wee Marquette emceeing and hustling the crowd without
shame. I don't remember going there after meeting Lester Young in
the cocktail arena. But I wanted to hear the live stuff, already mourning the days when the early innovators with each new set broke open
the mind and drove the heart and gut to a musical beyond.

John and Shirley came to town once in a while and took me to
see Marian McPartland at the Hickory House, a brass and chrome
piano lounge on upper Times Square. We sat around the bar with
our bourbons, nodding up at her on the piano platform. She'd play
her swinging efficient jazz with its subtle quotes from all the greats,
inside her own humble stabs at originality. She chatted a bit between sets, responding to Shirley's cute insider hip chatter and frank
appreciation. She'd talk admiringly, Shirley did, of the great "gone"
chicks in jazz these days. Yes, Marian herself and "Neets" O'Day. She
was a heartbreaker, my new sister-in-law, with her lost girl hipness
and her lonesome heart craving initiation into the "gonest" jazz
mysteries. I recall that later, when she turned forty, she announced,
"I'm a forty-year-old Dizzy groupie." Bop was our mutual creed.
How could I not love her?

But the Hickory House was a tepid scene. It was so clearly cocktail digging, strong and competent as it was. It was ice-in-the-glass
highball jazz and it ended early and somehow was meant to. From
there you went on to steak dinners, late theater, and after-dinner
parties. John and Shirley probably did just that. I went home a little
tipsy—not much—and played some bipolar Bud Powell and went to
bed on the cusp of a lost thrill.

It was that fall when I began talking to a girl named Susan Berg-
man in the cafeteria. I'm not certain of anything about Susan except
that bebop was her *raison d'être*. She was short, mostly because she
hunched her shoulders—thin with black curls falling around her
face. She wore dark-rimmed glasses (everybody did) and had black
eyes that shone out of a pretty, mousy face. No beauty, but cute and
half-grinning a lot as if everything was *going* to be funny even if it
wasn't now. She was the only girl I met in college who was a real

"chick." She was hip, but not cool. She followed the bop scene. She was avid and exclusive. She didn't truck with any other interest, though I think she was an English major. She was Jewish and lived in Hell's Kitchen—way west by Tenth Avenue in the forties, and she dated *only* black guys. And she dug *only* black bop.

The guy she hung around with that fall was an Adonis—tall, lithe, cream-coffee-colored with the kind of lips, eyes, nose, and facial structure that come at you from those Greek statues—the cold blank look of physical perfection. I mean, even when he smiled—a row of white dazzle—you stopped dead at the graceful lips, perfect teeth, slender nose, pristine eyes—all of this brown gorgeous harmony vitiating any message there might be behind it. Perfection murdered the imagination and made an iceberg of the heart. Not Susan's, though. She clung to the guy like a maniacal fly that would affix itself to the eye socket of the Belvedere Apollo. When he walked into the cafeteria with his head high, skimming above the student swarm, Susan was dashing around him from elbow to elbow with her half-grin showing a fetching little overbite, like a privileged gnat. You felt he could swat her away if he wanted to, but he was too sublime and accepted her as his court. He wasn't very affectionate with her. He was a black Adonis, after all, and if you couldn't turn the head of the most beautiful white girl in the room (probably Jean Nussbaum with her swooning white swains from the film department), it would confirm your own beauty to have this cute, hip little white gnat buzzing at your elbow and hanging on your words. And coffee-brown as he was, it upped Susan's currency, which was marginal and narrow at best, to play the attendant courtesan to a guy who *everybody* recognized— even if you couldn't proclaim it—as a god.

I don't remember his name. He didn't talk much to me when I began sitting at their table. The truth was, he didn't talk much to Susan either. He moved and swayed against the back of his chair. With his hands in his pockets, his broad shoulders in the draped jacket waved alternately as if to the smoothest tenor in town—as if he were always hearing Lester Young lilt through an old standard. He looked around, spotting the scene, but never really connecting with it. Then he'd angle himself up, and looking over her head, say, "Got to go. Hey, Bobbie-girl, I'll dig you later. Maybe we can get something going this weekend. Hey, girls." A slender hand flips behind him as he glides off. So gone and isolated in an iron cocoon of beauty. Susan would blink and grin and titter across to me. "Isn't he just the *most*! I mean," and she'd pause to giggle and throw me a private wink, "What else can I say?" as if we, and she generously included me, were the favorite wives at a noble unattainable black court.

Oh, there were the established kings and queens and their courts in the room—the maniacal Beat King and his ragged courtiers; the enchanting Jean whose coffee was always brought to her by running film boys; for the English types, the beautiful couple Peter and Ursula, like blond boy and girl sibling lovers, who fingered each other's hands at the table and laughed and gazed under fluttering lashes, ravishing children playing at love. Many were moonstruck around them. Naomi adored them and shamelessly paid court. "Byron and his sister—they're a poem in the flesh!" She'd gush away about pre-Raphaelite raptures and whisper hoarsely to me, "They're both queer, I'm sure of it. I tried Ursula at a party—a deep kiss, you know. She didn't balk—*definitely* not!" But try as all these tables did to attain royalty, to be the first among nations for fashion and desirability, they could never get the right aloof tone. They were too loud and chummy, too gregarious, too damn aware of each other. No, Susan, and me too, at least for the moment, attached ourselves to the black god who glided through the room looking above the swarm and moved in a true royal altitude. The remaining inhibitions of the white crowd, dotted as it was with token blacks, set off Susan's idol and conferred his godhead. Yes, I stuck with Susan for a while that last semester.

I went to her house one afternoon. I think she had a younger brother. The rooms were cluttered, crowded, and dingy. Her parents were not far above poverty. They worked, she worked, and by scrabbling so, they afforded a college girl. Life in the noisy drab warrens of Hell's Kitchen was not rosy. But she half-grinned with a quiet underground excitement. For some reason she was admitting me to her private little sub-continent. She didn't expose her dreary home to many from Washington Square. My other Jewish friends lived in well-appointed, respectable apartments in the Bronx and Queens, and Naomi herself in a brick complex with playgrounds and park benches in Sheepshead Bay, Brooklyn. But here was Susan living among struggling actors and ghetto Hispanics, with fire escapes like shoelaces tying up the buildings and huge ash cans clanging inside iron fences on the sidewalks. She was a cute little subterranean, and the first thing she did was take me into her cubbyhole room and put a Charlie Parker on the turntable. I barely said "hi" to her parents before she dragged me there and said, "Maybe we can double some-time. Bill" (we'll call him) "knows lots of guys—not from school. We can dig some sounds and go to parties up in Harlem where they live. You'd dig it, Liz." Her low tone insinuated up to me. She so much wanted a pal in these inky waters she was swimming in, and as noth-ing was happening, I didn't mind.

So I went out with a pal of Bill's. The four of us went to the Royal Roost and ironically enough were caught stomping to Char-lie Ventura, an old white honker. There wasn't much around. I went out alone with this pal a few times. He was a nice fellow, incredibly ordinary, and I don't remember his looks at all, or his talk, or his body. He never connected it with me. I suppose he just wanted to walk down the street or into clubs with me: pale public pleasures were all I was good for. But he *was* nice and tried to show me a good time. I think I liked jazz more than he did, and when I saw that Art Tatum was at the Three Deuces as we walked down Fifty-second Street, he very gallantly led us right in.

It was jammed—a long narrow room and the piano way off in the distance. From there, the crowd packed tighter and tighter as it neared the door until it was spilling out on the sidewalk like beer foaming out the neck of a bottle. It seemed a mostly white crowd, and we stood four rows deep behind the bar, our beers sloshing to us over shoulders. People talked and laughed—greetings passing from group to group. They were clearly excited to be here in the presence of the pianist Fats Waller long ago called "God." They were here to pay obeisance to the old jazz past, to acknowledge history and fame:

"We saw Art Tatum on Fifty-second Street before he died." They were not discoverers, initiates. They were not hip. It was noisy with the electricity of celebrity. In the distance, I heard myriad white notes like the flakes of a blizzard filling the air. I couldn't see the man at all. But the notes fluttered through the air, landing in my eyes and crawling up into my ears. They were white lights that shattered a stream of sound that ran ceaselessly underneath the indifferent, agitated crowd. Maybe it *was* God's strange luminous singing, and everybody had come to the advent and not listened. It was the weirdest jazz experience I had ever had—and after one set packed to the gills in the neck of the bottle and beer foam like sticky air all over my hands and tangling my hair, all competing with those airy notes for the heart of me, I wanted to split fast. Bill's pal didn't care. He just smiled a lot—the essence of pleasant without feature. He would do most anything or just as willingly do nothing at all.

These were odd featherweight times, my forays into the black scene with Susan and Bill. I could say it was dreamlike, except that dreams—the ones that stick with you—abound with sharp sensations. Details may be surreal and senseless, but the weird connections explode with a physicality that translates at once into extremes of emotions. You crawl tightly through a tunnel—blackness and heaviness crowding you—you *breathe* fear, you *see* hope as a pinhole of light ahead.

Postmortem effects—jazz was certainly not dead, and consorting with blacks *was* carrying on. If anything, my social life under Susan's exclusive, peculiar penchant was blacker than ever. But the bloom was gone—piano jazz and retread white honkers like Flip Phillips. Blacks were black or brown or whatever, but the street and club and restaurant scene was attenuated, a good sharp whiskey rinsed with water in a weary, midtown, rip-off cocktail lounge. No sullen furious stares, no knives, razors, guns, no Bird with a silver wing flying through the roof. Susan's black gang rounded the old sharp edge that had sliced sex into me on my mother's cot with Roy I and that had slashed death through my soul outside Le Downbeat with Roy II. No, everything with these nice guys, and girls too, was faceless and dreamy. We slid along the streets around Times Square in a dim glow. Everything friendly, everything easy, everything filmed away from contact, a hard cock encased in a rubber. We walked into clubs, restaurants—and—so what? Shrink-matted over with Bill's friend's brown film, I couldn't feel either white or black disdain touch me, though it was probably there—this was only 1953, after all. So off-kilter it all was. I actually missed the fury that was always on the edge of violence, sex, and murder of my early "black" years. A shriveled appendix of crusader still stuck to me, but there seemed damned little use for it those days.

"Hey, you wanna catch Stan Kenton at St. Nicholas Arena? There's a show Saturday night." "Sure!" So a few of us black and tans straggled up "there" some place and packed ourselves onto a lit up, enormous floor that throbbed with feet thudding thunder under mixed-colored bodies all in the throes of fake hysteria. I had a Stan Kenton record and had briefly fallen under his spell—the pride of cacophony, the beatitude of noise. And here it was in the flesh—and all egged on and manhandled by a fair-haired, loose-jointed skyscraper-of-a-leader who looked like the friendly golfer next door in Levittown. Except that he was crazy. Somewhere along the way he had discovered discord and had gone off the bat. Before, he had oozed on the soft edges of bop, writing and playing suites that wavered on the border between jazz and classical and finally lost themselves there. Then he must have heard the secret rumble of the oversized band in front of him, and, well, it was apocalypse time. There were Maynard Ferguson, Don Lamond, and a host of rabble-rousers, all the rumorous thunder of the universe about to explode—and suddenly he must have been giddy with power and taken his baton like a sword and set about liberating the noise of the cosmos.

Caught inside the vortex of this youthful, unsubtle, savage swarm, we stomped our way to the front row where we stood with our elbows on the stage, gaping up at the lanky blond Zeus with his thunderbolts. Blaring through "Peanut Vendor," Kenton lunged and swirled all around the stage, his arms like windmills gone berserk. He grinned out above us, a mouth jammed with big teeth, then at the guys standing up like ramrods in the bandstand, passing their barely managed blare up from tier to tier. Finally, before the last chorus, he glared down on us, jerking his open palms up, up, for us to stomp and shriek him on his joyride to heaven. Goddamn! For a minute Stan Kenton could make certain crowds—puzzled by bop complexities, bored by classical stuffiness and contemptuous of the current Top 40—believe that paradise itself was engulfed by upwelling ecstatic noise controlled by God's very own bandleader.

That night at the St. Nicholas Arena in black Harlem, itself held under the tyranny of the white god, was quite an experience. Trouble was, it blotted out realities. Dates, companions, group solidarity, even our little "I's" were brutally excised by the screeching heaven of Ferguson's trumpet and Don Lamond's chthonic booms from hell until I felt suspended, all the warm personal colors of life blanched away in a cold white heat. I never got any closer to Susan's gang that night in Harlem. When we staggered out to the street, Bill's friend was just as out of focus as ever. Those were curious evenings that didn't nourish much personal racial connectedness. Whether on Fifty-second Street or St. Nicholas Avenue, few borders were breached. No sex, no pounding at the gates.

★ ★ ★ ★

I tried to cover my bored desperation to get away from 681 that fall. But slinking up to my fifth-floor aerie of gloom was taking its toll. By now, my last semester, the fall of 1953, even the ghosts were gone. I couldn't even dredge up a serious haunt—John smoking and declaiming through tight lips from the wing chair, mother playing solitaire on the card table, Roy and Val bedding me down, Jack listening to Red Moscow, Virginia and Alan gone, Marian and Yael gone, Kitty with her knots gone, and all taking their genial comforting ghosts with them. And that left me—studying, wandering the little rooms, my music an echo, myself becoming the leftover wraith of 681. Oh, it wasn't the hungover angst of last spring. No terrors. No, unlocking the door day after day (or night after night as the case might be), the transformation began with the click of the tumbler, and I entered the ancient familiar tomb of my late adolescence with all its used-up, pockmarked props sadly in place: John and Marian's yellow paint cracking in the hall, the blue cover on the fornicating cot threadbare at the end where Kitty rested from her lustful futilities, the glass ashtray on the scratched cut-down table filled with only my lipsticked Chesterfield butts, the dresser on which to my ghostly eye the roaches skulked where in the early days they used to race with all the vigor of Portuguese explorers. No fear here on my entrance. All the props greeting me with the broken hearts of the dying. Postmortem effects: were we all, myself and my gentle friendly props, at the point in dying where fear drains away? I had to get away at times.

So enter Gene Mannheim from the scandalous English Novel course and a lover of *Tristram Shandy*. He was a comical fellow, tall, thick with a square face and strands of sandy hair combed across a balding head. Thick glasses widened his face. Every feature broadened the square, the lips always stretched tight exposing only the lower half of upper teeth in a perpetual grimace, which covered all the bases from smile to grin to laugh. His pink hands flapped open to his sides, his tone was sibilant and stagey—you imagined Noël Coward at your cafeteria table—his wide feet in black shoes toed outward, and with the dark overcoat draped to his shins, he was a sardonic penguin flat-footing his way toward you. You giggled at his approach. He deflected your good humor with ironic put-downs masked as affection. "Ah, is it Miss Holmes, who covered the history of the English novel from *Moll Flanders* to *Sons and Lovers* with nary a stop in between? My most ingenious crammer."

Gene had appointed himself the genial chair of our pre-final cramming sessions. With my disastrous skipping of most of nineteenth-century British fiction, I had been unable to cough up even the most rudimentary plots of those endless novels. He patted my shoulder with pink fingers and grimaced warmly in my direction, a large cuddly penguin of ambiguous sexuality. He liked girls all right and was the particular friend of a sharp-tongued brunette, also from the novel course. But she read all the books, was genuinely amused

by them, took them in the light social spirit they purveyed, and got
an A. But I had at least one credential to throw at him:"You're wrong,
Gene. *Wuthering Heights* stopped me dead. In fact, I ignored most of
the questions and wrote two pages in the blue book on Heathcliff
and Kathy. So there!" "Ah yes, ever on the search for grand passion
and brutally rolling over all tender entertainments on the way. But
we all love you anyway," he grimaced again and patted my hand. We
shared Eda Lou Walton's modern poetry class that last semester where
I fared better with the passions of Yeats and Hart Crane, and we both
thoroughly enjoyed the Village and Taos gossip that tickled the fading
lady so. We would both get As without much trying.

If he was Noël Coward on the cafeteria stage with his s's and
lilting and lingering tonalities, there could be a fugitive warmth in
private. The voice lowered and sentence endings were clipped, eyes
sharpened and focused behind the lenses, the grimace turned serious. At such private turns, you realized with surprise that Gene had
shadowy levels of awareness. "Well, Liz, if you want to get away from
that lonesome, roach-infested, solitary walk-up cell for a weekend,
you're welcome to vacation in the Mannheim roach-infested suite
with bars on the window in the old-fashioned, homey Broadway
Central Hotel, loved domicile of exiled students of WSC."

I had often talked of my odd solitude at 681 Lexington, trying to
euphemize that weird dungeon of isolation under the skylight. Gene
read the message on that shadowy level of his where he read so many
of the secrets in the air around him. During the week, he lived at
the Broadway Central Hotel, a grand, ornate flophouse, because he
lived too far out in Jersey to commute (some faraway ocean town
like Perth Amboy). He often went home on the weekends, though it
was hard to imagine him there in some high, frame house common
to ocean country, sitting at the breakfast table with dour, forlorn
parents hovering over him with eggs and flapjacks, orange juice, and
the Amboy Sunday paper. Would his hisses drop off and his tonalities deepen and monotonize? Would he hide his shadows and dot
his i's and cross his t's and talk about his girlfriend? I wondered, why

did he go, and so regularly too? He became serious and sentimental
over his parents, "They're very sweet, you know. Quite proud. They
never push me to come. But we all tear up when I leave on Sunday.
I couldn't possibly not come. Hearts would break." That was that.
One of his speeches you dared not giggle at.

"Can I really stay there, Gene?" I asked him one afternoon,
referring to his lively sordid room at the Broadway Central. "I
could use a change of scene. Besides, maybe I could crash one of
the Beat boys' parties."

He told them at the front desk that a friend would be staying
Friday and Saturday nights in his room and told me to pick up the
key there. They were prepared, he stated, "Though this is a casual
hostelry where protocol is not an issue. You will be welcomed or ignored in the amiable, nonjudgmental fashion of this historic Broadway landmark. There's a bottle of booze, so kick up your feet and
regard the bricks through the bars on the window and enjoy your
freedom!" he instructed.

I walked over to Broadway from Astor Place, then down a block
or so to the Central on the west side of the avenue. The beginning of the warehouse district—heavy square monsters, maybe ten
to fifteen stories high, with big wide dirty windows facing out
between blocks of gray stone, like the swollen cheekbones of a
prize fighter, that are scarred and bisected by gray-green girders.
Trucks backing in and out of ground floor, corrugated doors that
flap up with a cackling shriek. Huge cartons and packing boxes everywhere—on forklifts, crowding the sidewalks, piling up behind
the large upper windows. Moving, storage, and commerce banging
and thudding behind the growling voices of drivers and stockmen.
Beneath the glamorous windows of Fifth Avenue emporiums, a
pristine silvery stream, lay this unseen riverbed of brutal warehouse boulders with all their crashing, bellowing underground life.
Lower Broadway, the ugly blood and bile and bones of business,
its hollow-eyed, grimacing skeleton, baring its true face. The sun
never made it down to these streets—the ever-grinding, invisible
digestive system of capitalism.

Today, of course, it's all dolled up in party dress—Broadway, Lafayette, Prince, Spring, East Bleecker—all the obese giantesses painted and rouged with fluttering colored ribbons up their fronts announcing galleries and high-end boutiques and bright clear window-eyes flashing in the afternoon sun that now chooses to dip down among the ten and fifteen stories and bless this new latte-land with its artrepreneurs and artisanal cheeses, this Soho square of the flamboyant very rich quilt that has now covered just about every corner of dear old ugly Manhattan.

In the days when I walked on lower Broadway or east of Astor Place or west on Twenty-third Street or under the El anywhere on Third or through Times Square, I was inside the gross, feral, naked, mechanical heart of the city, the great clanking black heart that bared its teeth and made it go. Then New York said to you, around most of its corners, "My heart is money and my blood is commerce and it's an ugly business—so, what're ya gonna make of it, bub?" A few designated areas were allowed to evade the issue—a pretty Greenwich Village set aside for kooks and perverts and bohemians with their beads and bars; a sedate Gramercy Park with its academies of poetry, its locks, and manicured white poodles; Sutton Places for Cheevers to write about. But the rest flaunted the pride of the deformed. Heavens, even those stately stone mansions of the Upper East Side were in a slump, broken up into rooming establishments with cracks here and there, peeling paint on a window-frame, a front door showing its age. And affordable for a short postwar hiatus. My sister and a friend lived in one for a time—in the east seventies—a block you can only trespass on these days. No, in those days the business of money didn't try to pawn itself off as something elegant and beautiful, not in New York at least. Where have all the grindings and clangings and packing boxes gone?

And so the Broadway Central—Fall 1953.

Friday afternoon—a plate of spaghetti and meatballs at Rienzi's on MacDougal—beer glasses on the stained, varnished wood table—jokes and gossip filtering through smoke and out the window into the dusty 4:30 p.m. sunlight on the street. Mouth bleeding with red sauce and large, dense balls rolling in my stomach like oversized ball bearings. Our crowd piling onto the jammed strip of sidewalk—some headed for Remo's—"God bless, Liz, and may he manifest his epiphanies to you in my monastic cell!" Heavy balls rolling me kitty-corner through the park, east. Delicious vagrancy among the packing boxes.

And so the Broadway Central—Fall 1953.

High ceiling—graying pressed tin—iron bedstead far below. Books in a case and stacked on top. Bedside table with radio. Bottle of whiskey on tall dresser across from bed. Furniture crouching low on thinning carpet of uncertain design, worn to the woof in the middle by the thousand feet of inmates, darkening to purple at the edges. Glass of lone gracious whiskey as the dusk settles down over the bricks out there—everything washed to gold, inside and out, by rye and sun. Sleep. How sweet this night-empty precinct, void of personality, indifferent to charm. So irrevocably away. Yes, Gene, a place to meet the blank face of God.

Here, now, the Broadway Central.

Morning—instant coffee from the two-burner on the table—high white walls bright without the sun—the bricks alight without the benefit of sky. Something unnatural fills the room with morning. A round Danish scored with sticky drips of white glaze, a navel of purple jam rising in its middle—my Saturday morning-eye of sun with black pupil to greet the day.

Lazy, poking among papers on desk by a window bathed in an odd sourceless light. No need of lamps to read the term papers and notes from Eda Lou's class, odd curlicues and caricatures in the margins, tiny renderings of the faded Village rose. Slipping so delicately into this alien friend's world like sliding through a half-opened door into a party and losing yourself in the dancers and the music. Retreat, withdraw, resurface in the privacy of the other. High empty light, peace and safety of another's privacy. Poking, puttering, nosing deliciously out of myself into another's artifacts.

Peace at the Broadway Central.

Shattered—outside now, splinters of light stab my face—diamond—points of clarity: Walking, half-running west along Waverley. High sun—a clear spotlight from the sky following around me as I dart across Fifth Avenue. It blares down over and under the Arch to sear through clothes and skin, scorching rib cage and burning away the heart-case to lay bare its contents—like breaking the hasp of the trunk and hurling its treasures to the hard floor to die of exposure. ("Sure, Liz, I'm free this afternoon—it'll be late when you get here. You can stay in the extra room. Too far to go back to the city tonight. See ya later.") Down two levels at the Fourth Street station to the double A train across Brooklyn, surfacing in Queens, all the way to Rockaway, the end of the line. An hour, my body shaking and slowly gyrating with the half-empty Saturday car—coming out in far sea light, strange land and bay formations—flat sandbars with roads zigzagging across the water in intricate patterns. I'm a refugee with satchel of clothes and books, waiting for the bus and the last half-hour leg of the exile's journey across the world to the small Hungarian enclave where my pal Charlie Baum will open his parents' house on the last spit of land to pierce the sea at Far Rockaway, Long Island, and the warm welcome of immigrants to the last escapee.

The words intone off the page in a sharp feminine voice: "I'm glad to hear that you've finally conquered . . . your revulsion for Liz. I remember how often you'd voice it. I quote you precisely."

Now a lilting sibilant voice, "I can't help it. I find her the most vapid, repulsive girl in the WSC student body. It is painful to be in her presence . . . ," falling tonalities, "but you see, I must fight this feeling, it is so clearly ignoble arising as it does from the vulgar precinct of the gut. But there it is, my dear . . . " Oh, the tired resignation, rising for the instant loudly in the half-empty car, "I will excise it and suffer her to haunt my room in my absence . . ."

And then "Good luck, my friend, in this experiment in laceration." The last word from the dark girl—mixing in the subway synthesizer, "revulsion, repulsion," echoing, rhyming, and finally submerging in the low steady crashing of the car—the specific sounds and syllables that had thundered through the head and landed like bombs on the heart all day—murdered at last under the metal wheels of the AA train.

I sat with Charlie in his room. He played some swing records and we talked of his favorite movie director, Vincent Minelli, and how much we loved his latest, *The Bandwagon*. We gossiped about Professor Gessner's recent seduction and his fingering himself in class. I ate globs of pork dumplings at his parents' table and went to sleep with the sounds of the sea coming through the window, "revulsion, repulsion" lapping in with the minor slipping of the waves—returning with the blank detachment of the sea—for the moment unrelated to me or Gene. Sounds, syllables, absurdity.

Sunday I went back—all the way, two and a half hours—around the globe to 681 Lexington Avenue—amazed at the million angles of myself the world held, able to exist in anyone's mirror, momentarily refreshed, forever damaged. Like life, in the face of all disasters, bombs, and weathers that it carries on its glossy, willy-nilly way, this brutal self-portrait was glossed over fairly quickly.

A postmortem dialogue with Gene: "Why didn't you stay Saturday night?" Silence, shoulder shrug, averted face. "Didn't feel like it . . ." Move away a bit.

His face clouded, stern. "You saw that letter from Margo."

Shoulder shrug. I feel the wound in my face.

"You couldn't understand. Margo and I have a private language. We communicate in hyperbole."

The wounded face says it doesn't matter.

"No, you don't understand. If the sky is a bit cloudy, I say to her, 'The sky is like a rancid, gray, disgusting diaper ready to let go a shower of piss on us,' and really, it's only a bit overcast."

All this explanation is clearly a brand of truth. In the wake of this possibility I feel the wound in my face fade into the cool gray of his cloudy sky. "It's okay, Gene. It really doesn't matter. I shouldn't really read other people's mail anyway."

He doesn't agree, is silent. This too is to his credit and his credibility. His hands flap to the sides in the old penguin posture, his eyes are clouded. I know he is sorry. We both seem to know that the little one-act drama between us is beyond resolution. Finally, there is explanation and truth, and there is effect and the two will never meet between Gene and me. "So long," and we sit a table or two away in the large English major clan in the cafeteria.

I finished the semester the way I began—businesslike—attending to curricula, papers, and exams, closing out love and comradeship along with studies. I holed up in 5D, not wishing for weekend escapes, finishing my paper on Robert Penn Warren and British cathedral architecture. By Christmas it was clear that I would get a full house of As. Even Gessner approved my work on *Red Badge* and renewed my faith in the integrity of his lust. No punishment if you don't make the grade in seduction. I was pulling away from entanglements beyond the most casual. Living even momentarily with the ugly portrait of myself had given me cold confidence. I recalled a Ginsberg revelation about being everybody's monster. It could be extended. Everybody is somebody's monster. How marvelous! I thought of Allen with affection, almost with the beginning of tears. Imagine! This odd profound old pal of John's was willing to be *everybody's* monster! If he could contemplate that, then I could surely settle into being just Gene's.

New Year's, 1954.

I went to the dullest party I had ever been to—a gathering of mostly black and some tans in a Sugar Hill apartment in Harlem. The jazz was at moderate volume, the talk was desultory and short-circuited, the dancing and swinging were subdued, the colorful faces didn't light up, the drinking was halfhearted, and the grass brought only low and intermittent laughter. People drifted through rooms, not connecting through space. Bill's friend took me home on a subway that was a minor riot of revelers with paper hats and whistles. I suppose he kissed me at the door, and I said, "Thanks, actually that was the only New Year's party I've ever been to."

Chapter 12

Leaving 681

—— I graduated in January 1954, just as I had from high school in January 1949, which means I didn't attend commencement. If you wanted all that folderol you had to hide yourself in the June class of 1954. You tagged along behind the year-end class, behind when you were really ahead, always on the offbeat. I've never worn a cap and gown, and I received my degree in the mail sometime in the spring when it was forwarded to my new address, Box 75, Old Saybrook, Connecticut. No ceremony, no handshake from the dean. No regrets. I was glad to be finished with it all. I didn't hang around the cafeteria after the finish the way I had around Rhodes in spring of '49, picking up people by the MoMA fence. I'd been learning a lot about endings, starting with John and Marian, Mom gone, Kitty gone, the Beat crowd with its music, its antics, its lusty, indomitable zeal of body and spirit, flown to the winds like older siblings who lose interest and stop guiding and guarding the youngest. And Gene Mannheim's startling verbal portrait of me—all had schooled me in the art of endings.

But there was one regret that hung about me like a shroud I was reluctant to throw off. "I'll need February, Mom, to get my stuff together. I have to see the head of the English department for recommendations for graduate assistantships for the fall. Give me another month, and I'll be ready in March." It was getting a bit tight for her, paying the rent at 681, but she agreed. There I was phonying up my rationale to her as I had done last summer for *leaving* the apartment—only now to linger on to the dead end of 681. I had a big box of records, another of books (not many as I had borrowed steadily from John's library for years. I didn't go to branch libraries and had never been in the underground stacks of NYU—John again), and one and a half suitcases of clothes. I could get them ready in a weekend. I had long ago had Professor Cargill write letters for me—my applications were in at a number of universities in the Midwest where teaching assistantships were said to be plentiful— Michigan, Iowa, Indiana—unheard-of spaces on the map, square blocks near the middle of the country that my imagination balked at the thought of actually living in.

I didn't know it, except in the cellar of the heart that knows everything, but I hated to leave 5D, 681 Lexington. Here, with my neighbors across the way in Lexington House, invalids and masturbators, with the comings and goings next door and now in 4C—oh, the grief of the forsaken 4C—with friendly roaches and the rented furniture— the living room cot, the cot with the stand and the music, the wing chair whose stories had become novels, the black table with glass bowl so abundant with butts like the dashes of a Kerouac book, *here* was the only home that had grafted itself to me. Oh, I didn't want to leave. My end-period love for the place engulfed me that February and, in a place too deep for consciousness, it broke my heart. I got cheesecake from the deli, picked up some evening newspapers, and sat around the apartment in a torpor. I'd sit looking at the card table where my mother played solitaire for hours at a time. I'd look at the wing chair and listen for voices. I'd play jazz (knowing that it would follow me everywhere) and look out the window, wondering if Charlie Parker or Wardell Gray would ever sound the same audacious, ravishing notes of discovery again without that special private window on the world. I moped and thought nothing—imagination of the future blanked out.

March came and my mother, perhaps John too, came into the city with the Packard. I don't recall any of the three or four trips it took to load me away. The only thing I do remember is some insistence about the black table. Since John himself had cut it down and brought out its inner curving loveliness, we thought we'd get away with carting it off. Good-bye, 5D, its furniture resting in place for the next itinerant. Good-bye, Lexington, its future in the ever-changing hands of the gods of Manhattan. I may have cried, but the trip out has no reality in my reverie. I somehow doubt it. We drove to Saybrook. I stacked my records in "my" little room and began moving toward the future. We went out to dinner. I must have seemed forlorn in spite of the talk about jobs and graduate study because Shirley said, "Listen, honey, any time you want to go to New York you can always stay at 123. We're going to hold onto it for a while."

And so they did, and so I did. One spring weekend I was puttering around her comfortable, homey place with a big coffee table and a huge glass ashtray and the phone rang. It was Jack Kerouac.

"Hi, Liz, what's up? I was looking for John. I'm in town on Long Island for a short visit to my mother. But how are *you*, Liz? It's so long ago . . ."

"Yes, Jack, it's great to talk to you. I hear such stories about all of you in San Francisco. I just finished college and I'm up in Saybrook until fall when I'll study and teach someplace."

"You're big now, Liz." He was quiet and faintly chuckling—the goofy surprises of life always touching him.

"Well, yeah, I'm twenty-one."

"You're the last one to leave Lexington Avenue. It's so strange . . ." voices trailing off—all's said. "Listen, if you're going to be there next week, maybe I'll get over to see you. It'd be nice, like old times."

But his voice said we wouldn't be reminiscing. He was talking to a young woman now, and for a second, it seemed that he wanted to make love to me. Only for a second. "Okay, I'll call again and come to see you." I didn't stay far into the week, and he didn't call and didn't visit 123. Something more than a rendezvous between Jack and John's younger sister, now grown-up, was over.

John and Shirley were solidly transferred to their made-over, rangy house behind my mother's Victorian. Their ample living room was the scene of much conviviality—a new brand, a mordant tone. The walls were clothed with books, the corners booked in, and on one wall at floor level records (vinyls now) stretched from end to end. On the opposite wall John had cut an enormous opening in which he had put a picture window fashioned out of odd, picked-up panels of glass. The mantle walls were open. On one side was a round yellow dish chipped on one edge showing a foreshortened Christ on the cross—his tiny childish arms are off the cross and hanging aslant of his sides, his graceful curving legs suspended—no nails, no straining hollow torso, no blood—a couple of cherubs peek from behind a decorative arch and columns, and there are blue curlicues and flowers on everything: a springtime Jesus born again on his cross, a sweet insouciant Christ posing under a marriage arch. Perhaps it is of Catalan origin. It is on the side of my mantle in Maine now.

There was also a large rectangular oil portrait of the Virgin and child, a solemn remote pose, Byzantine in tone, but blackened, somber, Russian. As you look in its direction, it startles and disturbs—the umbrous wood frames a window into a brooding medieval eastern century. There it sits casting its impassive, pitiless eye into your space. It hangs over my mantle now in my library, which is also clothed in books, one wall containing six lower bins of vinyls. Someone said it was the genuine article among a lot of broken antique flotsam and jetsam handed down from my mother. "That's really a prize." I looked at it and agreed and said nothing. John had actually fashioned this prize, faithfully copied it from some medieval source and out of the Russian side of his soul. He had varnished and shellacked, and aged it in Shirley's oven and chiseled the grooves in the blackened wood frame. But the piece de resistance of the house was the bar in the living room. Over it John had cut a hole in the wall to the kitchen for the easy passage of booze. Over the hole he had mounted a pastoral print in ornate frame. He had hinged its sides and sawed the picture in half. So he would open the scene and Shirley would pass bourbon through the hedgerows of England.

Then two facing threadbare sofas and two easy chairs at the ends formed a ring of conviviality. All of this seating was often filled with a new crowd from New York. Heavy drinking as before, cigarette packs littering the fine low oak table that stretched between the sofas like a wide bed of pleasure—the glasses, the bowls of nuts, the thin roaches at the ready for their moment, two ample brass bowls with rising cones of butts like live magma. This was a new crowd in their thirties, men with revolving, pretty girlfriends, people who were perhaps in publicity or owned bars in midtown, with new names now: Jerry Garderian, Stuart Fenton (lovely man), Jim Harelson. I'd be invited occasionally when I passed through Saybrook on my rambles. I was old enough, had been around, and with drinks could banter pretty well, keep my end up just above the square line.

There was much laughter—laughter largely *at* the world and *of* the world at which it laughed. These were sharp guys who took the pulse of the world moment to moment and pronounced it, with wit and high hilarity, sick—and the ultimate hipness was to eat of the sickness and laugh instead of puke. John would later call this "the glittering upper world," or at least a spin-off of same, and he would struggle to write a book about it. And they *were* attractive and enormously funny, and I enjoyed the evenings enough to drink plenty of the booze that came through the picture that was cut in half and opened as a window to the kitchen—flowed through, a golden stream of whiskey—and smoke the roaches along with the filtered Kents we were all smoking now.

John, with largesse and a growing girth (though they were perennially poor and fed themselves on mammoth stews and neck-bone soups), kept the booze and talk flowing, urging people to higher and higher peaks of wit. Jim Harelson was an idol of hip, so hip that he could get away with square, and the convolutions would enthrall everybody until they laughed all the way to despair. Shirley adored him and called herself his "groupie." They'd all travel periodically to St. Louis where they would continue to put down the world with their originator and stage producer, Jay Landesman, in his own Crystal Palace. John went too—after all, that city was where Shirley had surfaced out of a bitter, funny, alienating childhood.

Yes, those were the nights when I would check in on my big brother and his new life. Of course, most of the time he was caring, thinking, fretting, writing, and drinking in the daily mission of his life. But
on these weekends when the gang would arrive from New York, the
edgy sarcasm flowed with the new week's material, the amber stream
carried it along, and behind it all John kept the phonograph revolving
with all the old geniuses and, often now, a lot of Clifford Brown and
Sonny Rollins—so much Rollins. It was back there behind the couch,
just loud enough to fill in any blanks between hilarities.

But there were few pauses in this black comedy of the world, and I
had to cock an ear to catch the bliss back there. I secreted my favorites,
and they *were* my bliss in that lovely idiosyncratic room. The zigzagging phrases of "Love Is a Many-Splendored Thing" hitching up,
then abruptly lying down in waltz time. The most lilting waltz of all,
"Valse Hot," Rollins' signature theme. The exuberant climb Sonny
takes us up into "The Way You Look Tonight" with Monk. By now
I'd learned a bit about how to fish and cut bait. I could laugh at the
latest Harelson outrage and smoke the roach and drink my fill of the
booze, flirt with Jim, and whistle the songs in my head—all in the
same coda. But Rollins was the only beat I took away from those
evenings of raucous destruction.

The world lay in square ruins at the end of these nights, killed by
some of its own modest successes. It seemed a marriage of discord.
The Beat had gone out of John's living room for me in these revels.
They were hip, they were mordant, they smoked pot, they did it all
to jazz, they laughed, and they slept around. But they didn't write
poetry or novels (except John, bless his true heart) or believe in the
beauty of cunt or live on petty change and roar across the land in an
old car, eating cheese sandwiches, and they didn't exult over visions,
and the last thought in their heads would be "Everything's always all
right." They looked at their watches and blew their minds in their
free hours, but they didn't know Neal's "time." I came away in a
depression of nostalgia. Yes, something was over—had fled to a new
coast and left New York in the hands of trends and trashers.

Epilogue

Spirit of Place

——— I spent the next ten years as an itinerant English teacher and full-time nomad. Yes, Indiana first where my comp student whispered in my ear in March of 1955, "Bird is dead," and then in the dead Bloomington air, "Bird lives!" because all I talked about that first year was bop, still not understanding the compositional techniques of organization and development. Then onto Michigan and Illinois. I cared just enough about money to bend it to my needs—for records, for an old car to take me back and forth—Midwest to East, on all-night runs, and from job to job. I quit for a year to wander around Europe on the q.t., on the hunt for adventure, to arrive in capital after capital with one suitcase filled with clothes and another with a typewriter (which I hardly used), in the evening off a boat in Athens, in Rome at a midnight Stazione Termini, in Paris, Gare de Lyon, midnight, Madrid, Barcelona—on the sly, no friends, no known hotel—always making my own way to find the *pensione*, the *trattoria*, cafe, bar—to find all of it and companions, as Ginsberg says of his closet door in "Transcription of Organ Music," to find all of it "kindly stay(ing) open for me." There were difficulties and hard times, but the world I sought graciously opened its arms to me so that I could once again, in the spirit of an earlier age and without the barriers of attitude or fear, eat of the tree of life.

Some of it was indeed bitter fruit, but if I dropped my armor and my demands, more of it was sweet. I had affairs—some serious, others casual, some short and tender, others short and forgettable. I rented furnished apartments—I had no experience of any other mode of living. I carried my belongings on my back. They barely filled the trunks of old cars—the books, records, phonograph, unused typewriter that held my deepest, unsung ambition. I played my bop in Bloomington, Indiana, in Alma, Michigan, in DeKalb, Illinois. I lost jobs and left jobs early and was modestly successful at others. I always found people to drink with and often ones to listen to jazz with. I had nightmares of loneliness and desolation and dreams of love and kinship of spirit. I found I did better when I banked on the adventure of life, something I had learned somewhere early on—in the beginning of consciousness in a place where my world began.

A few times every year of what is now a long life, I have a dream of place—what Lawrence called the "spirit of place," only decked out in the flesh of detail. It is always a contemporary dream that follows me through the decades. Sometimes I am walking up the sacred way of Lexington Avenue from Grand Central on the east side, past the new glass towers, the cruddy barren chain eateries, the luggage shops, upscale hotels, the T.G.I. Friday's on the corner. Then I'm at a beat-up door to a dirty vestibule that kindly opens for me—no keys, no buzzers, no magnetic cards—and the inner door opens, too, at my touch, and the shadowy stairs slant up to one dim hall above another as before—past 4C, oh, yes, which I don't stop at—until finally in amazement I'm at the top and there's a light from the half-opened door to the roof. I'm thirty, forty, fifty, sixty, and I can't believe my good fortune in this newfangled emerald city where you can only live on gold. It's 5D and I walk in and everything is there—cot, chair, card table, little desk by one window—and there is light from the skylight. My room is there facing its back world. Often I will set about rearranging furniture, finding ways to fit in new sofas, one here, one there, coffee table, chairs in corners, trays of food coming in from the hall kitchen. Food and drink. I realize that someone has been paying the rent for decades, for all my life, waiting for me to arrive at last. What luck, what undreamed-of possibility! A place to live in this modern, unlivable city—*the* place just for me, kindly waiting for me to live in once again. I'm wild with gratitude and excitement. I plan a party. Time to celebrate. I am setting out once again from my first home at 681. Some things are never over.

I wake up in Tokyo or Paris or Ireland, in DeKalb, Chicago, and finally in Maine—and I am cheered.

Glossary

DEAN ACHESON (1893–1971). Politician and secretary of state in the administration of President Harry Truman from 1949 to 1953. Led American foreign policy in the Cold War. Designed and signed the NATO pact for the United States.

SHIRLEY ALLEN (1928–1988). Married John Clellon Holmes in 1953 and resided with him in Old Saybrook, Connecticut. The couple had no children.

WILLIAM BARRETT (1913–1992). Professor of philosophy at New York University and editor of *Partisan Review* from 1946 to 1953. Barrett authored *Irrational Man: A Study in Existential Philosophy* (1958).

MAX BECKMAN (1884–1950). German painter interested in the tragedy of human life. Ten of his paintings appeared in Nazi Germany's Degenerate Art Show of 1937, more than any other artist.

BIX BEIDERBECKE (1903–1931). Jazz cornet player and pianist of the 1920s, Beiderbecke worked with Frankie Trumbauer, the Jean Goldkette Orchestra, and the Paul Whiteman Orchestra. Compositions of note include "In a Mist," "Candelight," "Flashes," and "In the Dark."

HARRY BELAFONTE (1927–). Jamaican-born musician nicknamed "King of Calypso" who popularized the Caribbean music style in the 1950s. Worked with Charlie Parker, Max Roach, and Miles Davis. Known for "Banana Boat Song" and his album *Calypso*, which sold over 1 million copies in 1956.

MARTIN BLOCK (1901–1967). Radio disc jockey who started to play music between news segments. Hosted "Make Believe Ballroom," which aired in 1935 in New York at WNEW, in which he purported to be broadcasting from rooms filled with live musical acts. In fact, he played records from a sound booth.

HARRY BRIDGES (1901–1990). Member of the Communist Party and president of the International Longshoreman's and Warehousemen's Union from 1937 to 1977. Opposed the Cold War and used aggressive labor tactics, causing many to call for his deportation.

BOB BROOKMEYER (1929–). Developed the idea of the concert jazz band and recorded albums with his New Art Orchestra. Continues to play with the same orchestra today at the New England conservatory.

EARL BROWDER (1891–1973). General Secretary of the Communist Party USA from 1932 to 1945. Was the party's presidential candidate in 1936 and 1940. In 1944 adopted the belief that capitalism and socialism could co-exist, a philosophy called Browderism.

CLIFFORD BROWN (1930–1956). Jazz trumpeter with a bebop and hard bebop style who was inducted into the Jazz Hall of Fame in 1972. Noted for avoiding drugs and alcohol.

GEORG BRUNIS (1902–1974). Jazz trombonist who could not read music but could play by ear and invent parts. Played at the jazz night-club Nick's in Greenwich Village in 1938 and from 1939 to 1946.

WILLIAM S. BURROUGHS (1914–1997). Avant-garde author, paint-er, and filmmaker of the Beat generation. Met Kerouac and Ginsberg at Columbia University in the 1940s; Author of *Queer*, *Naked Lunch*, and many other novels.

PUPI CAMPO (?–?). Latin jazz orchestra leader who played with Tito Puente. Known for a more mainstream jazz sound.

WILLIAM CANNASTRA (1922–1950). Muse for some Beat generation artists; died jumping out of a moving subway. He appears in John Clellon Holmes' *Go* as Agatson and in Jack Kerouac's *Visions of Cody* as Finistra.

LUCIEN CARR (1925–2005). Roommate of Ginsberg in the early 1940s who fatally stabbed David Kammerer in 1944. Kerouac assisted him in disposing of the knife. Carr served two years in prison as a result. The event is recounted in Kerouac's *Vanity of Duluoz*.

NEAL CASSADY (1926–1968). Inspired the Beat generation's free-flowing style of writing through letters sent to Kerouac. Served as in-spiration for the main characters of many Beat novels. Had a sexual relationship with Ginsberg and was a member of Ken Kesey's Merry Pranksters documented in Tom Wolfe's *Electric Kool-Aid Acid Test*.

CHARLIE CHAPLIN (1889–1977). Comedy actor, mime, and clown. Wrote, acted in, and directed silent and sound films, such as *City Lights* (1931), *Modern Times* (1936), and *Limelight* (1952). His signature character wore a thin mustache, big shoes, tight overcoat, large pants, and derby hat.

KENNY CLARKE (1914–1985). Jazz innovator of bebop drumming style, including the "ding-ding-da-ding" pattern for which this style is known and pioneer of the bebop combo. Nicknamed "Klook" for his snare and bass drum improvisations.

MONTGOMERY CLIFT (1920–1966). Film actor who starred with Elizabeth Taylor in *A Place in the Sun* (1951). Also starred in *From Here to Eternity* (1953) and *The Young Lions* (1958). Nominated for an Academy Award for Best Actor for his role in *The Search* (1958). He and Marlon Brando were known as the "Golddust Twins" because they became famous early in their careers.

AL COHN (1925–1988). Jazz saxophonist and one of the "Four Brothers." Wrote songs for "The Andy Griffith Show" and "The Pat Boone Chevy Showroom." Composed and recorded more than 100 original tracks.

EDDIE CONDON (1905–1973). Jazz musician and bandleader who played the banjo, guitar, and piano and also sang. One of the innovators of the Chicago Style of Dixieland jazz. Played regularly at Nick's in Greenwich Village.

NOËL COWARD (1899–1973). English actor and playwright. Wrote the popular operettas *Bitter Sweet* (1929) and *Cavalcade* (1931). Starred in American TV specials in the 1950s with Mary Martin.

NAT KING COLE (1919–1965). Jazz pianist, singer, and songwriter who formed the King Cole Trio, remarkable for its fusion of blues and jazz styles with bouncy vocals. Hosted a musical variety show on NBC in 1956.

MARY COLUM (b. Mary Gunning Maguire 1884–1957). Irish literary critic. Married Padraic Colum in 1912. Served as poetry reviewer for *The New York Times Book Review* in the 1940s.

PADRAIC COLUM (1881–1972). Irish poet, novelist, biographer, folklorist, and friend of James Joyce. Taught briefly at Columbia University.

HARTE CRANE (1899–1932). American poet. His poetry features archaic language and combines English literary tradition with American literature à la Walt Whitman. Kerouac and Ginsberg read his *The Bridge*. Committed suicide by jumping off a steamship.

TONY CURTIS (b. Bernard Schwartz 1925–). Actor of the 1950s and 1960s who was renowned for his thick, wavy, black hair, Curtis appeared in such films as *Some Like it Hot* (1959) and *Houdini* (1953).

MILES DAVIS (1926–1991). Jazz trumpeter, bandleader, and composer who was involved in the development of bebop, cool jazz, modal jazz, and jazz fusion. He is known for using a heavy vibrato on his trumpet.

RUSSELL DURGIN (?–?). Renter of the apartment at 321 East 121st Street, Harlem, New York, in which Allen Ginsberg experienced his William Blake illumination in 1948, detailed in his poem "Howl."

ALLEN EAGER (1927–2003). Cool jazz and bebop saxophonist and one of the "Four Brothers." Collaborators include Fats Navarro, Wardell Gray, Max Roach, and Terry Gibbs.

GERHARD EISLER (1897–1968). Acted as a liaison between the Communist International and the Communist parties of China and the U.S. In 1948 he was described by *Newsweek* as the "Number One Red Agent" in the United States.

ROY ELDRIDGE (1911–1989). Jazz trumpeter of the Swing Era nicknamed "Little Jazz" whose style influenced bebop. Used harmony with tritone substitutions, high register lines on his trumpet, and rapid double time notes that were followed by regular pace.

T.S. ELIOT (1888–1965). American-born literary editor, essayist, playwright, and poet. Believed that poetry should represent the complex nature of modernization. Best known works include *The Wasteland* and *The Four Quartets*.

MAYNARD FERGUSON (1928–2006). Played the trumpet, flugel horn, and valve trombone during the big band era. His recording of "Gonna Fly Now," the theme of the film "Rocky," received three Grammy nominations.

BUD FREEMAN (1906–1991). Jazz tenor saxophonist. One of the original members of the Austin High School Gang of 1922, which innovated the Chicago Style of jazz ("Nicksieland"), a version of Dixieland that features the string bass, the guitar, swing-style, solos, and is faster paced than traditional Dixieland.

AVA GARDNER (1922–1999). Gardner was a model and actress. Named "The World's Most Beautiful Animal" in the 1950s. She was married three times: to Mickey Rooney, Frank Sinatra, and Artie Shaw. Nominated for the Academy Award for Best Actress for her role in *Mogambo* (1953).

ERROLL GARNER (1921–1977). African-American jazz pianist and composer who bridged the gap between nightclub and concert-hall jazz. Known for spontaneous vocalizations while performing and for sitting on a telephone book because of his short stature. Composed "Misty."

STAN GETZ (1927–1991). Jazz saxophonist who played in Woody Herman's Second Herd from 1947 to 1949. One of the band's four saxophonists, dubbed "The Four Brothers." Won a Grammy for Best Jazz Performance of 1963 for his song "Desafinado."

DIZZY GILLESPIE (1917–1993). Jazz trumpeter, composer, and pioneer of the bebop and Afro-Cuban styles of jazz. Nicknamed "Dizzy" for his crazy on-stage antics. Known for using a trumpet bent at a 45-degree angle, which created a unique sound, and for having prominently puffed-out cheeks when he played.

IVAN GONCHAROV (1812–1891). Russian writer whose novel *Oblomov* (1859), featuring a young nobleman who can barely leave his divan, is considered a satirical vision of the Russian aristocracy.

BENNY GOODMAN (1909–1986). Dubbed the "King of Swing," "Patriarch of the Clarinet," "The Professor," and "Swing's Senior Statesman," Goodman was a jazz clarinetist.

DEXTER GORDON (1923–1990). One of the first bebop tenor saxophonists and a film actor. Nicknamed "Long Tall Dexter" because of his 6'5" stature. Known for his "large and spacious" sound and for reciting the words of ballads before playing them.

BRAD GOWANS (1903–1954). Pre-bop jazz versatile musician, Gowans played the trombone, clarinet, and cornet. Played at Nick's in Greenwich Village and with notable jazz musicians such as Bobby Hackett, Bud Freeman, and Max Kaminsky.

WARDELL GRAY (1921–1955). A western-style bop tenor saxophonist and clarinetist notably not into the drug scene. Encouraged other young musicians not to pursue drugs as a way to enhance their music.

DAVID LLEWELYN WARK (D.W.) GRIFFITH (1875–1948). American film director of the first feature length American film, *The Birth of a Nation* (1915), which presented the Ku Klux Klan as heroes of the pre-Civil War South and black slavery as favorable. Created racial controversy. His next film, *Intolerance: Love Through the Ages* (1916), was an unpopular silent film that presented racism as the intolerance of differing viewpoints.

BOBBY HACKETT (1915–1976). Played trumpet, cornet, and guitar in Dixieland style. Covered Bix Beiderbecke's "I'm Coming Virginia" in 1938, becoming known as the "new Bix." Played with the Glenn Miller Orchestra from 1941 to 1942.

AL HAIG (1924–1982). One of the pioneers of bebop and the first white bebop pianist, Haig was part of the original nine musicians to record the first session of Miles Davis' *Birth of the Cool*.

GUS HALL (1910–2000). Leader and presidential candidate of the Communist Party USA. Part of the "Little Steel" Strike of 1937, in which the nation's smaller steel manufacturers tried to unionize themselves.

ALAN HARRINGTON (1918?–1997). Novelist and friend of Kerouac and Ginsberg, Harrington wrote *Doctor Modesto* and *The Secret Swinger*. He is embodied in the character Hal Hingham in Kerouac's *On the Road*.

BRET HARTE (1836–1902). American author and poet who wrote excitedly of pioneering in California. Starting in 1868, edited *Overland Monthly*.

COLEMAN HAWKINS (1904–1969). Renowned jazz tenor saxophonist who brought the instrument to the forefront of the genre. Nicknamed "Hawk" and "Bean." Participated in the first bebop recording in 1943 with Dizzy Gillespie and Max Roach.

ROY HAYNES (1925–). One of the most recorded jazz drummers, Haynes plays in a variety of styles, including swing, bebop, jazz fusion, and avant-garde jazz. Nicknamed "Snap Crackle" in the 1950s for his expressive style.

BILLIE HOLIDAY (1915–1959). One of the greatest and most emotive jazz singers in American history. Songs such as "Strange Fruit" and "God Bless This Child" became building blocks of early American jazz music. Received her nickname "Lady Day" from Lester Young in 1936.

HERBERT HUNCKE (1915–1996). Thief and drug addict who stored stolen goods in Ginsberg's apartment. Reportedly coined the term "beat" to Kerouac to describe the generation. Kerouac passed the term on to John Clellon Holmes, who cemented its use in his novel *Go*.

MILT JACKSON (1923–1999). Jazz vibraphonist with a hard bop style known for his twelve-bar blues at slow tempos. Jackson was also a singer and pianist and played with the Modern Jazz Quarter.

ILLINOIS JACQUET (1922–2004). Jazz tenor saxophonist, bassoonist, and improviser with the famous solo "Flying Home." Introduced the honking tenor sax to jazz, a sound which later influenced rock and roll.

JAMES P. JOHNSON (1894–1955). Pianist, composer, and one of the inventors of the stride style of jazz piano playing. Wrote the hit song "Charlieton." Influenced such jazz musicians as Art Tatum and Thelonius Monk.

DUKE JORDAN (1922–2006). Bebop pianist and composer who played piano in a quintet with Charlie Parker, Miles Davis, Max Roach, and Tommy Potter. Wrote the bebop classic "Jordu."

MAX KAMINSKY (1908–1994). Jazz trumpeter and bandleader of the Max Kaminsky Orchestra. Known for his Dixieland style. Played for the Original Dixieland Jazz Band. Collaborated with Tommy Doresy, Artie Shaw, and Bud Freeman.

STAN KENTON (1911 or 1912–1979). Jazz pianist. Leader of the Stan Kenton Orchestra. In the forties, his sound was influenced by Latin rhythms. In 1950, started the Modern Music Orchestra, an innovative thirty-nine-piece group. Mixed swing styles with classical orchestral numbers.

DON LAMOND (1920–2003). Swing drummer who played in Woody Herman's First and Second Herds. Worked with Boyd Raeburn and Charlie Parker. Selected for George Wein's Newport All-Stars in the late 1960s.

JAY LANDESMAN (1921?–). Beat writer and poet. Knew Allen Ginsberg and Jack Kerouac. Owned an art deco bar called the Crystal Palace in St. Louis in the 1950s. Published and edited the Beat avant-garde magazine *Neurotica* from 1948 to 1951.

SUSANNE K. LANGER (1895–1985). American philosopher who specialized in linguistic analysis and aesthetics and studied with Alfred North Whitehead. Author of *Philosophy in a New Key: Symbolism of Reason, Rite, and Art* (1942). Lecturer at Columbia University from 1945 to 1950.

PEGGY LEE (1920–2002). Singer, songwriter, and actress who performed with Benny Goodman to record songs such as "I Got It Bad and That Ain't Good" (1941). Starred in the film *Mr. Music* (1950).

GERSHON LEGMAN (1917–1999). Author of *Love and Death*, which attacked American sexual censorship and repression and claimed graphic violence replaced the act of sex in pop culture. Also the publisher of *Neurotica*, a Beat counterculture journal. Credited with coining the phrase "make love, not war."

MAX LERNER (1902–1992). Journalist with a liberal political and economic view. Editor of multiple publications, including *PM*, a New York City newspaper devoid of advertisements and their special interests, which he joined in 1943.

HAROLD LLOYD (1893–1971). Actor who starred in a number of comic short films in the teens and early twenties. Began feature film work in 1921 and also produced a number of films throughout his life.

ROGER LYNDON (1917–1988). Professor of mathematics who attended Harvard in the 1940s and taught math at Princeton.

NORMAN MAILER (1923–2007). Novelist and essayist. One of the originators of the New Journalism style of writing. Author of numerous books, including *The Naked and the Dead* (1948), and of the controversial essay "The White Negro" (1957). In 1955, along with Ed Fancher and Dan Wolf began publication of *The Village Voice* in Greenwich Village.

DODO MARMAROSA (1925–2002). Began his career as a pianist at age fifteen with the Johnny "Scat" Davis Orchestra. Known for combining swing and bebop styles, he recorded such jazz classics as "A Night in Tunisia," "Moose the Mooche," and "Yardbird Suite."

HOWARD McGHEE (1918–1987). Noted bebop trumpeter from 1945 to 1949. One of the first trumpeters of the era to play in the foreground of songs.

MARIAN McPARTLAND (1918–). Jazz pianist and violinist and host of *Marian McPartland's Piano Jazz* on NPR. Played at the jazz nightclub the Hickory House in New York City from 1952 to 1960.

LAURITZ MELCHIOR (1890–1973). Danish-American opera singer once defined as a baritone, Melchior came into his career when recast as a tenor in 1917.

VINCENTE MINELLI (1903–1986). Hollywood director considered the "father of the modern musical." Famous works include *An American in Paris* (1951), *Brigadoon* (1954), *Kismet* (1955), and *Gigi* (1958). Married to and divorced from Judy Garland. The father of performer Liza Minelli.

MIFF MOLE (1898–1961). Jazz trombonist and bandleader. Formed a band called Miff Mole and His Little Molers in the 1920s and another named Miff Mole and his Nicksieland Band in the 1940s.

THELONIOUS MONK (1917–1982). Jazz pianist and composer with an improvisational style, Monk is considered one of the fathers of be-bop. Known for his dramatic use of silence and rests and his abrupt splayed-finger poundings on the piano.

BREW MOORE (1924–1973). Jazz tenor saxophonist who played at the Roost and Bop City in New York in the 1940s. Later moved to California. Recorded many original tracks, including "Fuguetta" and "Lo Flame."

ANITA O'DAY (1919-2006). White American jazz singer from Chicago. Worked with Gene Krupa, Stan Kenton, and Woody Herman. Often associated with West Coast Cool jazz scene. Affectionately called "Neets" O'Day by jazz devotees.

CHARLIE PARKER (1920–1955). Jazz alto saxophonist of the 1940s central to the creation of bop music. Nicknamed "Yardbird," Parker developed a reputation for his fast-paced improvisations. Worked with Dizzy Gillespie in small ensembles.

HENRY BAMFORD PARKES (1904–?). Author and history professor at New York University from 1949 to 1972. Wrote *A History of Mexico*.

FLIP PHILLIPS (1915–2001). Played the tenor sax and clarinet and co-led a group with Bill Harris that was at the heart of Benny Goodman's music groups. Often received uproarious applause after improvisational solos.

BUD POWELL (1924–1966). Bop pianist and composer who mentored Thelonious Monk in the early 1940s. Plagued with mental problems after 1945, which stemmed from racially motivated police brutality in Philadelphia.

PEREZ PRADO (1916–1989). Cuban bandleader and composer known as the "King of Mambo." His music from the 1940s through the 1960s was part of the first Latin music to garner American interest outside the Latino communities.

WILHELM REICH (1897–1957). Austrian psychiatrist, psychoanalyst, and scientist who discovered "orgone energy," which he believed to be the universal life energy. Reich built orgone accumulators to harness the energy, believing that sitting in them would alleviate illness. William Burroughs researched and wrote of orgone energy, hoping that the accumulators could cure withdrawal symptoms from heroin, and built a chamber. In *On the Road*, Kerouac refers to an orgone accumulator as boosting the sex drive.

SONNY ROLLINS (1930–). Tenor saxophonist influenced by bebop. Acquired the nickname "Newk" from Miles Davis because he resembled a Brooklyn Dodgers' pitcher Don Newcombe. Known for unaccompanied solos on the saxophone.

PEE WEE RUSSELL (1906–1969). Jazz clarinetist and saxophonist. His style consisted of squeaks and overtones, an early example of free jazz. Known for the mournful facial expression he wore while performing.

GENE SHARP (1928–). Author of numerous books on political theory. Theorized that the success of political power lies in the extent to which the subjects give power to their leader(s) through obedience; change can be exacted when people nonviolently withdraw their obedience. Director of the Albert Einstein Institute in Boston, Massachusetts.

GEORGE SHEARING (1919–). Blind jazz pianist and composer who played in an all-blind band in the 1930s. Wrote the classic "Lullaby of Birdland." Played at Birdland, a jazz club in New York. One of his performances is described in Kerouac's *On the Road*.

JOHN "ZOOT" SIMS (1925–1985). Jazz tenor and soprano saxophonist. One of the "Four Brothers." Played with Al Cohn at a New York club "The Half Note" in the 1950s and 1960s as "Al and Zoot."

MUGGSY SPANIER (1906–1967). Cornet player and bandleader. Led several Dixieland jazz bands, most notably Mugsy Spanier and his Ragtime Band, which played traditional jazz with a swing rhythm section.

JESS STACY (1904–1995). Jazz pianist of the Swing Era. Famous primarily for a 1938 Carnegie Hall performance with Benny Goodman in which he played a solo of the song "Sing, Sing, Sing."

EDWARD STRINGHAM (?–?). New York friend of Kerouac. The inspiration for the character named Ketchum in *Go*.

SIDNEY TARNOPOL a.k.a. SYMPHONY SID TORIN (1909–1984). White radio personality. Known as the first man to play bop on the radio, particularly WJZ out of New York City. Would often broadcast live from Fifty-second Street jazz venues. Helped make the careers of jazz legends such as Charlie Parker and Billie Holiday.

ART TATUM (1909–1956). Jazz pianist who was blind in one eye with only partial vision in the other. Most noted for recording in a new style, breakneck tempo, in which his finger dexterity was highlighted.

BILLY TAYLOR (1921–). Jazz pianist and composer who played with Ben Webster's Quartet in New York in 1944. Pianist at Birdland. Musical director of NBC's 1958 television program *The Subject is Jazz*.

DYLAN THOMAS (1914–1953). Poet, short story writer, and film writer who read his works on the radio with a striking voice. In 1953 Thomas, a native of Wales, toured the United States, reading at forty universities. Thomas died from either pneumonia or brain disease in New York during this tour.

LENNIE TRISTANO (1919–1978). Jazz pianist and composer of Italian-American heritage. Blind from birth. Played in cool jazz, bebop, post-bop, and avant-garde styles of jazz. His wholly improvised "Intuition" and "Digression" are among the first documentations of free jazz style.

FRANKIE TRUMBAUER (1901–1956). Played the C-melody saxophone. Musical director of the Jean Goldkette Orchestra. Known for his collaborations with Bix Beiderbecke, with whom he created some of the most innovative and memorable jazz music of the 1920s.

CHARLIE VENTURA (1916– 1992). One of the first musicians daring enough to incorporate bop into his music. His band played a commercial form of the new jazz music of the time.

THOMAS "FATS" WALLER (1904–1943). Organist, pianist, and composer. Had a Broadway hit in 1929 with the song "Hot Chocolates." Also wrote "Ain't Misbehavin'" and "Honeysuckle Rose," both in 1929 and both inducted into the Grammy Hall of Fame.

EDA LOU WALTON (1894?–?). Poet and English professor at New York University who lived in Greenwich Village with author Henry Roth in 1927. Roth dedicated his book *Call It Sleep* (1934) to Walton.

ROBERT PENN WARREN (1905–1989). Poet, novelist, and critic. One of the founders of New Criticism, which was prominent in the 1920s to the 1960s. Best known for authoring *All the King's Men* (1946) and *At Heaven's Gate* (1943).

MAX WERNER (b. Alexander Schifrin 1901–1951). A German Social Democrat who was against fascism and capitalism.

GEORGE WETTLING (1907–1968). Dixieland jazz drummer who played with notable musicians such as Artie Shaw, Muggsy Spanier, Bud Freeman, Jess Stacey, Eddie Condon, and Billie Holiday.

BILLY WILLIAMS (1923–1986). Radio disc jockey for WNEW who hosted *Make Believe Ballroom*. Developed the show's catchphrase "Hello, world." Often provided personal anecdotes on the air. Nicknamed Frank Sinatra "Chairman of the Board."

ALAN WOOD-THOMAS (1920–1976). Artist who described out-of-body experiences in which he painted his works; known mostly for his female nudes. Was a friend of Kerouac, Holmes, and Ginsberg, and lived in Greenwich Village.

LESTER YOUNG (1909–1959). Jazz tenor saxophonist and clarinetist nicknamed "Prez" by Billie Holiday. Played sophisticated, relaxed harmonies rather than the popular "honking" style. Established the "hipster" style of the era. Known for wearing a pork pie hat.

Bibliography

Bennett, Robert. *Deconstructing Post-World War II New York City: The Literature, Art, Jazz, and Architecture of an Emerging Global Capital.* New York: Routledge, 2003.

Breines, Wini. *Young, White, and Miserable: Growing Up Female in the Fifties.* Boston: Beacon Press, 1992.

Caldwell, Mark. *New York Night: The Mystique and Its History.* New York: Scribner, 2005.

Carnes, Mark C. *The Columbia History of Post-World War II.* New York: Columbia University Press, 2007.

Cassady, Carolyn. *Off the Road: My Life with Cassady, Kerouac, and Ginsberg.* New York: Penguin, 1990.

Charters, Ann. ed. *Beat Down to Your Soul: What Was the Beat Generation?* New York: Penguin, 2001.

_____. ed. *Jack Kerouac: Selected Letters 1940–1956.* New York: Viking, 1995.

di Prima, Diane. *Memoirs of a Beatnik.* New York: Olympia Press, 1969. Reprint, New York: Last Gasp Press, 1988. Reprint, New York: Penguin Books, 1998.

Ellis, John. *World War II: A Statistical Survey: The Essential Facts and Figures for All the Combatants.* New York: Facts on File, 1995.

Frazer, Brenda (Bonnie Bremser). *Troia: Mexican Memoirs.* New York: Croyton Press, 1969. Reprint Champaign, Illinois: Dalkey Archive Press, 2007.

Freeman, Joshua Benjamin. *Working-class New York: Life and Labor Since World War II.* New York: New Press: Distributed by W.W. Norton, 2000.

Glassman, Joyce (Johnson). *Come and Join the Dance.* New York: Antheneum, 1962.

Gould, Alan E. *Post-World War II Price Trends in Rent and Housing in the New York Metropolitan Area.* New York: U.S. Department of Labor, Bureau of Labor Statistics, Middle Atlantic Region, 1967.

Grace, Nancy M. and Ronna C. Johnson. *Breaking the Rule of Cool: Interviewing and Reading Women Beat Writers.* Jackson, Mississippi: University Press of Mississippi, 2004.

Harman, Carter. "New Jazz Trends in Night Clubs." *The New York Times.* Section 2, X5. August 24, 1947.

Holmes, John Clellon. *Displaced Person: The Travel Essays.* Fayetteville: University of Arkansas Press, 1987.

_____. *Go.* 1952 Rev. ed. New York: New American Library, 1980; New York: Thunder's Mouth Press, 2002.

_____. *The Horn.* New York: Thunder's Mouth Press, 1988.

_____. *Nothing More to Declare.* New York: Dutton, 1968.

_____. *Passionate Opinions: The Cultural Essays.* Fayetteville: University of Arkansas Press, 1988.

_____. *Representative Men: The Biographical Essays.* Fayetteville: University of Arkansas Press, 1988.

Johnson, Joyce. *Minor Characters: A Memoir of a Young Woman in the 1950s in the Beat Orbit of Jack Kerouac.* Boston: Houghton Mifflin, 1983; Reprint, New York: Washington Square Press, 1990. Expanded ed. New York: Penguin Books, 1999.

Johnson, Ronna C. and Nancy M. Grace, ed. *Girls Who Wore Black: Women Writing the Beat Generation.* New Brunswick, New Jersey: Rutgers University Press, 2002.

Jones, Hettie. *How I Became Hettie Jones.* New York: Dutton, 1990.

Kerouac, Jack. *On The Road.* New York: Harcourt, Brace and Company, 1957.

_____. *The Town and the City.* New York: Viking Press, 1950.

Kerouac, Joan Haverty. *Nobody's Wife: The Smart Aleck and the King of the Beats.* Berkeley, California: Creative Arts Books, 2000.

Kerouac-Parker, Edie. *You'll Be Okay: My Life With Jack Kerouac.* San Francisco: City Lights Books, 2007.

Knight, Brenda. *Women of the Beat Generation: The Writers, Artists and Muses at the Heart of a Revolution.* Berkeley: Conari Press, 1996.

Landesman, Jay. *Rebel Without Applause.* London: Bloomsbury, 1987.

Lawrence, David Herbert. *Studies in Classic American Literature.* New York: T. Seltzer, 1923.

Legman, Gershon. *Love and Death.* New York: Breaking Point Press, 1949; New York: Hacker Art Books, 1963, 1985.

Metalious, Grace. *Peyton Place.* New York: Messner, 1956.

Peabody, Tim. *A Different Beat: Writing by Women of the Beat Generation.* London: High Risk Books, 1997.

Polomar, Normal. *World War II: America at War 1941–1945.* New York: Random House, 1991.

Population of New York City 1940–1948. New York: Consolidated Edison Company of New York, Inc., 1948.

Quintanilla, Luis. *Franco's Black Spain.* New York: Reynal & Hitchcock, 1946.

Rudolph, Kurt. *Gnosis: The Nature and History of Gnosticism.* Robert McLachla, ed., trans. San Francisco: Harper & Row, 1987.

The Simon and Schuster Encyclopedia of World War II. New York: Simon & Schuster, 1978.

Shulman, Alix Kates. *Memoirs of an Ex-Prom Queen.* New York: Knopf, 1972.

Skerl, Jennie, ed. *Reconstructing the Beats.* New York: Palgrave-macmillan, 2004.

Von Vogt, Elizabeth. *The Adventures of Dorothy and Marian.* New York: Writers Club Press, 2000.

_____. *An Awful Intimacy.* New York: Writers Club Press, 2002.

_____. *Brothers Under the Skin.* New York: iUniverse, Inc., 2003.

_____. *Cass Willey Leaves.* New York: iUniverse, Inc., 2005.

_____. *The Marriage Martyr.* New York: Writers Club Press, 2001.

This book is set in Bembo Regular 11/14.